THE
FACTS ON FILE
D-DAY ATLAS

THE
FACTS ON FILE
D-DAY ATLAS

THE DEFINITIVE ACCOUNT OF THE
ALLIED INVASION OF NORMANDY

FIRST EDITION

by
John Man

Facts On File®

AN INFOBASE HOLDINGS COMPANY

Facts On File, Inc.
460 Park Avenue South
New York, NY 10016

CIP available on request from Facts On File

Facts on File books are available at special discounts when purchased
in bulk quantities for businesses, associations, institutions or
sales promotions. Please call our Special Sales Department
in New York at 212/683-2244 or 800/322-8755.

Text design by Malcolm Swanston and Andrew Stevenson
Jacket design by Peter Gamble
Composition by Swanston Publishing Limited, Derby, England
Manfactured in the U.S. by Quebecor Printing Book Group, Westwood, MA
and Brattleboro, VT

10 9 8 7 6 5 4 3 2 1

ISBN 0-8160-3137-1

Printed on acid free paper

Contents

○ **Foreword – A Recollection**

On a hot summer's afternoon in 1944, a three-year-old boy was playing with a tennis ball in the narrow road outside his home, a cottage in a Kentish village. There was no traffic to disturb the quiet. Petrol was strictly rationed and the family car, a Morris, was on blocks in the garage. The boy kicked the ball across the road. It fell into the shallow ditch. The boy followed and climbed down to retrieve it.

At that moment he heard a noise, a steadily increasing roar. Something was coming. He looked down the lane and saw a motorbike with a side-car. He waited for it to pass. The driver waved, the boy waved back. Behind the bike was another and another and dozens more; and then trucks, all painted the same dirty greens and browns, open trucks with soldiers in the back. They, too, waved at him. The boy watched, amazed and awed, as the wheels rolled by and the men waved; and then frightened because the thought that went through his mind was that he couldn't get home for tea.

I was that boy and this was my first memory, still vivid after 50 years. Perhaps it was the week before D-Day, when troops were being taken to the camps from which they would embark. Perhaps earlier, when teams were storing equipment in side-roads and fields. In any event, I was just one of thousands of children who stood watching and waving at such convoys winding through the lanes of southern England that summer, preparing for the greatest amphibious assault ever, the assault that would eventually roll up the German empire in the west.

The memories of those children, reinforced by hearing about, and then reading about, those who fought, lived and died, soon became part of a much wider experience, linking millions. The build-up to D-Day, the day itself, the campaign that followed, the whole monumental operation has entered the psyches of many nations – Britain, America and France, of course, but also Canada, and to a lesser extent of other occupied nations contributing to the liberation forces. It is also an integral part of German history.

The events retold in this book reverberated across the world and down the years, in anecdote, history, photograph and film, echoing now into the third and fourth generations. These are not merely historical events. They are deeply personal to thousands who still remember them vividly. Even if you were not there, if you did not see the convoys, if you were not born, the chances are that you can still find some connection with those who played a part in the campaign.

As I did.

My wife's father, Charles Christian Wertenbaker, was a war correspondent reporting for *Time* magazine, joining 9th Division with photographer Robert Capa for the advance on Cherbourg. When I started work on this book, I came across his account of the advance, recorded in one of the first "instant" books, *Invasion!* His view, partial and close-up and soon out of print, includes details easily buried by the business of distilling events into history:

"One could be carried away by sentiment and say that the oppressed French welcomed their liberators with tears of joy, but that would not be the whole truth … The people of this part of France were not hungry, as many of us had thoughtlessly expected them to be. Calvados is rich in milk, butter, cheese, eggs, beef, veal, cider, applejack and horseflesh, and the countrymen are sturdy and long-lived … The Germans who occupied Calvados were not ruthless to the people … the wars of 1870 and 1914 had left people without the bitter personal hate of the Germans other Frenchmen felt … When the Americans and the British came, therefore, the people did not welcome them with unmixed joy. At first, when the bombs rained down and shells poured in from the sea on their town, villages and fields, crumbling their houses, destroying their cattle, killing and wounding many people … they wondered if it would be to any good purpose. They were afraid the invaders would be driven back into the sea …

Later, when they saw the masses of men and weapons streaming through the countryside and looked up through the dust at the skies full of zebra-striped planes, they decided the Allies were there to stay ... The welcome they offered then, as they waved from the roadsides and took wine to thirsty soldiers in the towns, was more real because it was tentative and restrained."

Reports like this were legion at the time. The flow of reportage, documents, accounts, diaries, reminiscences, photographs and film that began then has never ceased. If gathered, it would fill libraries and take lifetimes to absorb. If told in depth, the story would be the equivalent of several national epics. So this is not – could not be – an "in-depth" approach. It can fulfil only a limited task, focusing on the cutting edge of the Normandy campaign, on the men, events and commanders who made the running.

This means there are many things omitted. Every phrase, every generalization hides a human world of suffering (and sometimes exhilaration). Every action – even "minor" engagements, too insignificant for mention in the most detailed military history – might become a peak experience for the participants, if they survived. Never again would they live with such intensity. If they died, their deaths spread ripples of grief through circles of families and friends. Each survival, each death touched dozens, perhaps hundreds. No one history can do justice to these events or be a memorial to add tho those along the coast of Normandy: the cemeteries, the regimental plaques, the gaunt ruins of German gun emplacements and the museums.

Nor is there much indication here of the immensity of the occupation that followed in the wake of the campaign itself, of the suffering of the French people, of the burden thrown upon German friends and families at home by the doomed efforts of their men at the front, of the equivalent campaigns raging in Italy, on the Eastern Front, and in the Pacific, let alone of the role played by the campaign in the formation of the post-war world.

At most, this is a recollection, in tranquillity, of the terrible realities that, 50 years ago, helped to make our relative tranquillity possible.

John Man
London, 1994

○ The Author

After reading German and French at Keble College, Oxford, with a post-graduate diploma in the History and Philosophy of Science, John Man joined Reuters and then went into publishing, becoming Time-Life Books' European editor. He is now an author and scriptwriter. His non-fiction books include *Jungle Nomads of Ecuador: The Waorani*, an account of an Amazonian Indian tribe with whom he lived in 1980–81.

In the early 1980s he made a television documentary series, *Survive*, on human endurance in extreme circumstances. Whilst working on the series he met the subject of his book *The Survival of Jan Little*.

Other books include *Stay Alive, My Son*, co-written with Pin Ya-Thay, detailing Thay's escape from the Khmer Rouge.

A frequent contributor to both *Time-Life Books* and *Reader's Digest* books, he has written widely on the history of World War Two.

○ The Consultant

Dr. John Pimlott is Head of War Studies, Royal Military Academy, Sandhurst. His many publications on military subjects include *The Gulf War Reassessed*, *The Battle of the Bulge* and *Vietnam: The Decisive Battles*

○ Key to Maps

National colors

British, Canadian and Commonwealth

American

French

German

Military Units/Types

⊠ infantry

⊟ armored

⎫
⎬ airborne/parachute
⎭

• artillery

⊠ motorized infantry

Size of Military Units

xxxxx		
☐ or	**ARMY GROUP A** RUNDSTEDT	army group
xxxx		
☐ or	**FIRST ARMY** BRADLEY	army
xxx		
☐	corps	
xx		
☐	division	
x		
☐	brigade	
III		
☐	regiment	
II		
☐	battalion	

example:

German 12 SS
Armored Division   12 SS
appears:

General Military Symbols

◠ ◠ mines (land and dump)

✈ airfield

↓↓↓ coastal defence battery

↓↓↓ heavy Anti-Aircraft guns

♂♂ light A-A guns

⊕ mobile gun

⌕ ⌕ machine gun post

➤ light machine gun

⌂ concrete artillery post

⬤ German resistance point

Symbols (continued)

◉ area of strong German resistance

⌕ radar station

✼ sites of bombing

⚓ sunken ship

✈ bomber

✈ fighter

✈ glider

⬯ airborne landing area

⬭ airborne dropping zones

➤ army movements

⇢ army retreat

Army Front Lines Time Phases

earliest ～   ～   ～ latest

Army Movement Time Phases

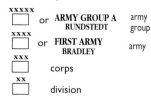

earliest   latest

Other Symbols used on Maps

● ○ town/village

⬢ built-up area

〰 major road

〜 minor road

⌁ track

▪━▪ railway

〜 river

〜 canal

⫶ bridge

swamp/flooded area

forest/wood

beach rocks

There was never any doubt about Churchill's intentions. "We shall go back!" he insisted to the House of Commons only hours after the British had been driven off the mainland of Europe at Dunkirk in June, 1940. At the time it looked like whistling in the dark. For a year Germany ruled almost supreme, balked of her final conquest in the West by British fighter pilots. Britain stood alone, bloodied, sapped, declining, with no possibility of vengeance.

Through the first half of 1942, disaster piled upon disaster. Hitler consolidated his rule on Europe, driving ever deeper into Russia. In Africa, the British were being forced eastwards into Egypt. In the Atlantic, the U-Boats sank Allied merchant ships at will. In the East, Japan had seized much of southeast Asia and threatened India, raising the specter of a link-up with German forces heading east through the Caucasus.

Yet in German success also lay the roots of Allied hope. Hitler's invasion of Russia in June 1941 forced Russia and Britain into unlikely alliance. Then after Japan attacked the United States navy at Pearl Harbor in December, Hitler too declared war on the United States, practically dictating American involvement in the European war as well as the Pacific one. By two unlooked-for chances, Britain had the world's two greatest nations as Allies. At the turn of the year, America committed herself to a vast build-up of her forces in Britain. Sometime, almost certainly, the British would go back.

But when? And how? Stalin demanded instant action – "The Second Front Now!" in the words of a popular catch phrase. But it was the two western

Weary British and French POWs are marched away from the beach at Dunkirk

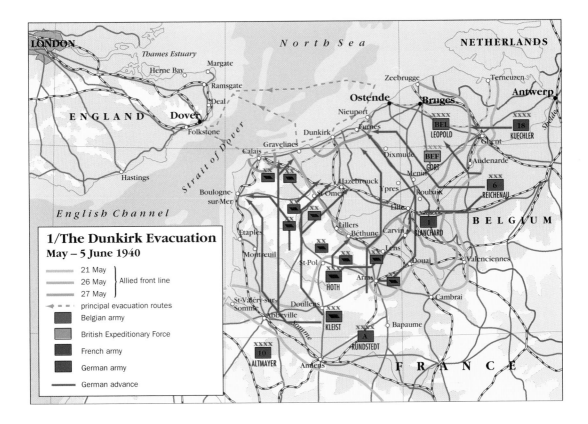

1/The Dunkirk Evacuation
May – 5 June 1940

- 21 May ⎫
- 26 May ⎬ Allied front line
- 27 May ⎭
- ◄- - - principal evacuation routes
- ▨ Belgian army
- ▨ British Expeditionary Force
- ▨ French army
- ▨ German army
- ── German advance

Allies who had to plan and attack, and they each had their own ideas about when and how. The most widely accepted British view was there could be no invasion without vastly superior forces. German weapons and tanks outclassed the British ones, its troops were seasoned and formidable. An invasion would have to be planned step by step, without committing to a fixed timetable. Better be safe and certain with a policy of slow strangulation than risk failure in a short, sharp strike. The Americans, on the other hand, saw no reason not to mobilize their immense resources, fix the day, aim hard and true for the heart of the Reich, and win. They wondered at the British penchant for prevarication, while the British tended to dismiss the Americans as naive and inexperienced.

There was some truth behind all these views. But there was a bottom line: Stalin desperately needed all the help he could get, and the other Allies needed to help him. If Russia collapsed, an army of three million would be

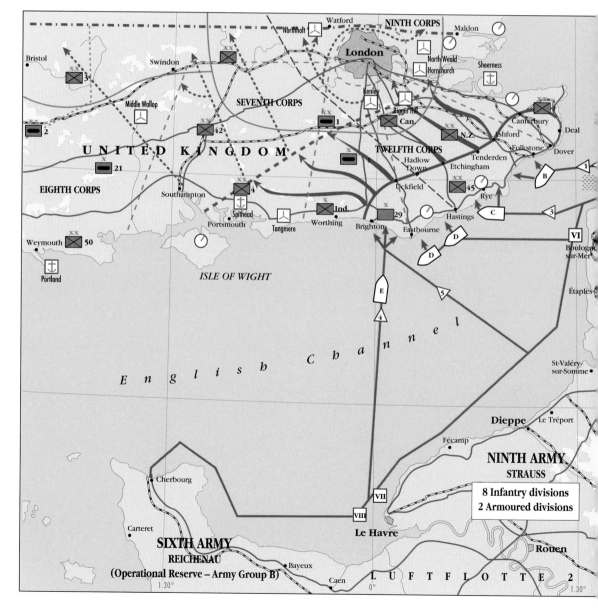

released for action in the west. If that happened, an invasion would become unthinkable.

All three Allies, therefore, were pushing in the same direction. Indeed, Britain had in small ways stated her intentions in action by sending commandos on several daring raids. In early 1942 the commando organization the Combined Operations Command, acquired a new chief, Lord Louis Mountbatten, who turned from morale-boosting adventures to the business of full-scale invasion. In the United States, Chief of Staff General George C. Marshall ordered emergency plans for the invasion of France, proposing a landing later that year to establish a bridgehead, with a second and larger assault in the Spring of 1943.

The British were hesitant. They suggested there should be an invasion of North Africa first. That was agreed by the Americans in the Summer of 1942. In return, the British agreed to a dress-rehearsal of the invasion. Everyone at

Some of the amphibious exercises undertaken by the Germans in 1940 in preparation for the planned German invasion of Britain

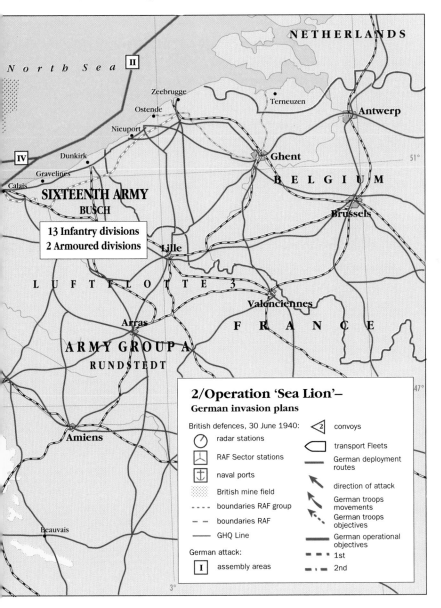

2/Operation 'Sea Lion'–
German invasion plans

British defences, 30 June 1940:

- radar stations
- RAF Sector stations
- naval ports
- British mine field
- - - - boundaries RAF group
- – – boundaries RAF
- ——— GHQ Line

German attack:

| I | assembly areas |

◁2 convoys

transport Fleets

——— German deployment routes

↖ direction of attack

↖ German troops movements

↖ German troops objectives

——— German operational objectives

- – – 1st
- – · – 2nd

Map labels: NETHERLANDS, North Sea, Zeebrugge, Terneuzen, Ostende, Antwerp, Nieuport, Ghent, Dunkirk, Gravelines, Calais, BELGIUM, SIXTEENTH ARMY, BUSCH, Brussels, 13 Infantry divisions, 2 Armoured divisions, Lille, LUFTFLOTTE 3, Valenciennes, Arras, FRANCE, ARMY GROUP A, RUNDSTEDT, Amiens, Beauvais

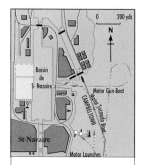

3/Raid on St-Nazaire
28 March 1942

The Normandy dock in
St-Nazaire was the only dock
on the Atlantic coast outside
Germany, capable of
accommodating the battleship
Tirpitz. The aim of this raid
was to destroy the dock and
its facilities.

⎯⎯⎯ track of
HMS Campbeltown
➤ ⸱⎯⸱⎯ track of Assault teams

In the morning of the 29 March
the explosives loaded into the
bow of HMS Campbeltown
exploded destroying the dock.

Canadian and British troops
march to a collection point
after the failed Dieppe Raid.
These men were then sent on
to prisoner of war camps in
Germany

that time accepted that the invasion would have to be launched through a major port. Mountbatten fixed on Dieppe.

The Dieppe Raid of August 19, 1942, had a number of aims. Besides rehearsing a sea-borne assault, the raid would test assault vehicles, probe German defences, capture prisoners and documents, and draw German forces away from the Eastern Front. In addition, it would give the Canadian army, 150,000 men camping under-used and bored in the English countryside, something to do.

The raid was a disaster. There was no preceding bombardment, in deference to the French population. In the approach, the raiders ran into a German convoy, and completely lost the chance of a surprise attack. On the flanks, commandos silenced clifftop batteries, but the beaches turned into killing-fields. When the 29 tanks came ashore, they were bottled up and picked off. Of the 5,100 troops who landed, 3,658 failed to return. Almost 1,000 men died, half of them Canadians. By comparison, the Germans lost under 300 men. The German High Command rightly concluded the raid was an amateur undertaking.

Nevertheless, the raid had a positive side. After Dieppe, Hitler was sure the Allies would launch the invasion proper against a port. On the other hand, the Allies now knew that if they did, they would fail. They also knew that surprise was vital, however hard to achieve. Pre-landing bombardment, specialized armored vehicles, landing craft designed to minimize casualties – Dieppe had none of these, and all would be needed in an all-out invasion. Mountbatten later wrote that each death at Dieppe saved 10 on D-Day.

In November, 1942, with British morale revived by their own successes in the desert, the Americans fulfilled their promise to invade North Africa with the largest amphibious landing to date. As the two Allied armies fought towards each other, Churchill and Roosevelt met in Casablanca. There, in January, 1943, the British got their way. There would be no invasion that year. Instead, the Allies would continue their push northwards from Africa into Sicily, and soften up Germany with a bomber offensive. Perhaps, as Churchill and the commanders of both the British and American bombing operations hoped, the bombers could actually force Germany to surrender without the need for an invasion. In any event, Churchill made a firm commitment: if there was no surrender, then the invasion would come the following year.

Planning started in earnest. There was as yet no commander of the operation, but at least it acquired a boss, Lt General Frederick Morgan, Chief of Staff to the (still-to-be-appointed) Supreme Allied Commander (COSSAC).

In May, the Allies set a date: May 1, a year hence. Six months later, the proposal had hardened. Stalin was told, and agreed. Now, whatever British misgivings, however exhausted the British economy was, there would be no turning back.

British apprehensions were well based. The German war machine was simply too strong. Weapon for weapon, man for man, they outclassed both the Americans and the British, even in 1944. In November, 1943, 4,000 Germans overwhelmed 5,000 British defenders on the island of Leros. Even after the stunning victory by Montgomery at El Alamein in October, 1942, it took three months – far longer than planned – for the two Allied armies to meet. In early 1944, the advance through Italy was stalled for four months, first at Monte Cassino, and again when the British tried to outflank the Germans with a landing at Anzio. As the weeks passed, the British remained nervous of an assault that, in early 1944, seemed a dubious enterprise.

Meanwhile, the build-up continued, under Morgan's leadership. COSSAC – Morgan's title, and by extension the title of his organization – tackled a task of unprecedented size and complexity. Based in Norfolk House, St James's Square, COSSAC's rapidly growing British and American staff set themselves a daunting goal: the defeat of Germany. That goal demanded a three-pronged approach: plans for a diversionary attack on the Pas de Calais to encourage the Germans to concentrate on the wrong place; plans for an instant invasion

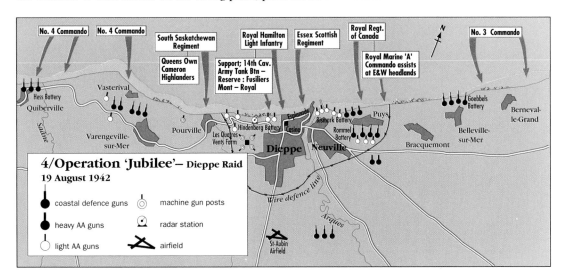

4/Operation 'Jubilee'– Dieppe Raid
19 August 1942

● coastal defence guns   ⊙ machine gun posts
● heavy AA guns   ⊡ radar station
◗ light AA guns   ✈ airfield

in case Germany collapsed; and Overlord itself, the full-scale invasion against a still determined foe. It was this last operation that increasingly dominated COSSAC'S work. It would take over a million soldiers, thousands of ships and tanks, millions of tons of supplies. No one knew how much, or where it would all come from, or when. The only fixed point was the date: May 1.

The first major tactical question to solve was where to invade. There was a mass of information on winds, tides, coastal defences, enemy troops, and airfields all along the 3,500 miles of coast from Norway to Spain. As a result of an official request broadcast by the BBC, the public sent in over 10 million holiday photographs and postcards, providing topographical details from which a specialist team at Oxford University drew up maps of astonishing accuracy.

In fact, the practical choice was much narrower than the full 3,500 miles. The overriding needs were firstly for beaches, and secondly for beaches that could be dominated by Allied fighter planes. The closer to Britain the better.

In addition, the invasion force would need to seize several ports through which the vast mass of men and materials could pour.

There were in the end only two possible sites: the closest, the Pas de Calais, and the Normandy coast near Caen.

As the closest, the Pas de Calais was at first glance the most obvious, and for that reason already heavily defended. At second glance, though, Calais was rather less suitable. Even without its heavy defences, its high cliffs, narrow beaches and small ports made it less than ideal.

That left Normandy, more weakly defended, still within reach of fighter cover, with broad beaches and a large port, Cherbourg, through which supplies could flow. True, the Channel was 100 miles wide here, but it faced the center of Britain's south coast, with its many fine harbors where ships could gather in force, and in secrecy. Morgan became certain this should be the spot, though it took until June, 1943, to convince Combined Operations Headquarters. Even then, the decision had to be confirmed. The swimmers and canoeists of the Combined Operations Pilotage Parties spent many nights on those beaches gathering sand samples to ensure the going was firm enough for heavy vehicles.

That, of course, was only the start of an immense and daunting planning operation. To take just one problem: how would the invasion be supplied and reinforced after the landings? Morgan, who had been told to plan for no more then three divisions, assumed it would take two weeks to capture Cherbourg. Meanwhile, the invasion called for the landing of some 12,000

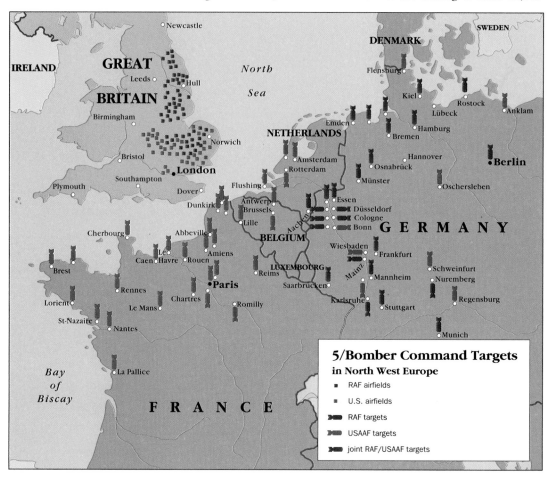

5/Bomber Command Targets
in North West Europe

- ■ RAF airfields
- ■ U.S. airfields
- ▶▄ RAF targets
- ▶▄ USAAF targets
- ▶▄ joint RAF/USAAF targets

A Boeing B-17 Flying Fortress
of the 91st Bomb Group, 8th
Airforce, flies low over the
town of Groisette, France,
January 1944

tons and 2,500 vehicles a day. To plan on delivering such a weight of equipment across open shallows was to court disaster. The Channel's weather was notoriously fickle, with good weather seldom lasting more than five days. These problems suggested an audacious solution: artificial harbors.

Churchill had proposed such a scheme back in 1917. Now he did so again, and COSSAC set about building two immense artificial harbors, known by their codename, Mulberries. These were to be made in sections, over 200 of them, the largest being barges some 200 feet long and 60 feet high, all of which would be towed across and sunk to form two harbor walls, themselves protected by 74 cargo boats and obsolete warships. To tow these unwieldly structures into position through high seas, winds and tides would take every heavy-duty tug on both sides of the Atlantic.

The disaster of Dieppe suggested further innovations. In the invasion proper, demolition of mines would have to be done by machines. A tank expert, Major General Sir Percy Hobart, was given the task of equipping a whole armored division with a variety of odd-looking tanks. These, the "funnies," would swim ashore supported by canvas "skirts," churn their way through minefields with chain flails, unravel their own coconut carpets from huge forward mounted bobbins to get themselves over soft ground, and turn themselves into bridges and ramps.

Dieppe had also shown the need for more effective covering fire. Bombing and shelling barrages from the sea were not enough. The assault forces would have to land with heavy guns, mortars and rockets ready for use. And the key to the whole landing would be the landing craft themselves, LST's, or Landing Ships, Tank. Some 3,000 would be needed. In the Summer of 1943, it did not seem there could possibly be enough of them. In Britain, new LST's took a quarter of all the steel used in ship-construction.

British equipment for European liberation. Long lines of Bofors light A-A guns ready at an equipment depot somewhere in southern England

These were a few of the grand issues. But such an operation also demanded the care of minutiae, like the amount of sacramental wine for pre-invasion communicants, and the numbers of condoms soldiers might need – not for the usual purpose, but as handy devices to stretch over rifle-muzzles to prevent salt water getting in, while keeping the gun ready for instant action (an idea that came to nothing).

Meanwhile, invasion planners also found themselves to be victims of differing Allied agendas, disputes that pointed to quite fundamental differences in long-term political objectives. Churchill still spoke of launching massive invasions along the south of France and the Balkans. The Americans suspected the British of ulterior motives, of hoping that Russia and Germany

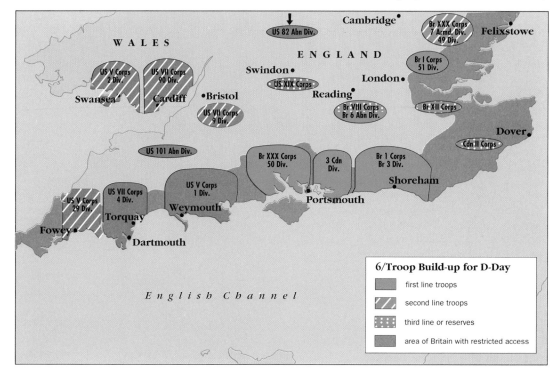

6/Troop Build-up for D-Day

- first line troops
- second line troops
- third line or reserves
- area of Britain with restricted access

British Prime Minister, Winston Churchill, talks to troops of the 101st U.S. Airborne Division as part of the "Churchill–Ike" tour in England on March 23 1944

would simply fight themselves to a standstill, leaving Britain to dominate an exhausted Europe. In their turn, the British accused the Americans of wishing to abandon Eastern Europe to Russia, and wondered at the Americans' apparent double-talk, planning for assault while actually being more interested in victory in the Pacific. At times, both sides doubted if the other was really serious about invading Europe at all.

In fact, during late 1943, the invasion of Europe seemed an increasing certainty, with an increasing possibility of success. As German victories were reversed, as the Battle of the Atlantic slowly turned in favor of the Allies, America geared itself to total war. Production rose, recruiting increased and men and materials poured into Britain. America might, after all, have 1.5 million men ready for the invasion, and Britain her planned 1.75 million. In addition, there would be 150,000 Commonwealth troops, and 40,000 from the occupied countries of Europe.

All this posed unprecedented problems to Britain's Victorian railway system, twisted roads and antiquated ports. The railway tunnels, for instance, were too narrow for tanks to be transported on flatcars. Cargo backlogged by bottlenecks in the English ports piled up in New York, so that eventually British imports had to be trimmed to allow the build-up to continue.

All this while, until the Autumn of 1943, COSSAC had been awaiting its SAC – its Supreme Allied Commander. Churchill had wanted to appoint a British officer. But as the Americans came to dominate the build-up, it was agreed the commander should be American. Roosevelt took his time. In the end, there was only one obvious candidate, Gen. Dwight D. Eisenhower . He had been in on the invasion plans almost from the start. Though his first battlefield command had been quite recent, in North Africa the previous year, he had a unique blend of military professionalism and diplomatic charm that proved vital in reconciling the conflicting demands of two governments, six services, and tough, demanding personalities too numerous to count.

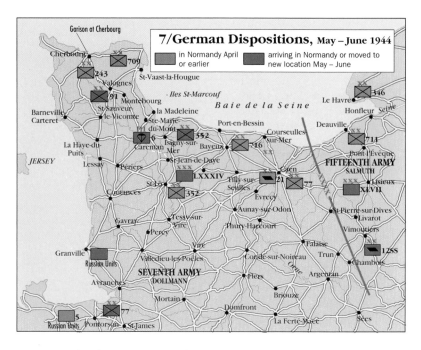

7/German Dispositions, May – June 1944

in Normandy April or earlier | arriving in Normandy or moved to new location May – June

General Dwight D. Eisenhower gives the order of the day – full victory or nothing – to soldiers of the 101st U.S. Airborne Division

In December he was appointed, and COSSAC became SHAEF, the Supreme Headquarters of the Allied Expeditionary Force. Eisenhower arrived in January and shifted the ever-expanding operation from central London to Bushy Park, near Hampton Court, creating a tent town of some 750 officers and 6,000 men. Here he could concentrate on the immense task ahead.

He had a talented and experienced team. His deputy was Air Chief Marshal Sir Arthur Tedder, former RAF chief in the Middle East and Eisenhower's colleague in the Mediterranean. Naval forces were under Admiral Sir Bertram Ramsay, planner of the North Africa invasion and the Dunkirk rescue. Head of the joint air force was Air Chief Marshal Sir Trafford Leigh-Mallory, veteran of the Battle of Britain and the Dieppe raid. Eisenhower brought in his own long-established chief of staff, Lt. General Walter Bedell Smith, and retained the invasion's original genius, Morgan, as deputy chief of staff. Ground forces were given to General Sir Bernard Law Montgomery, abrasive and egocentric, but a hero to the British after his victories in North Africa.

Quickly, old plans changed, amidst considerable and often rancorous controversy. The three divisions for the assault were raised to five. They would attack on a broader, 59-mile front, spanning the coast from Caen to the Cotentin Peninsula. The western beaches, though, gave on to cliffs, valleys and flooded areas, with restricted – and vulnerable – crossing-points to the interior. It would take a powerful airborne assault to secure them.

The greatest disagreement was over the question of bombers. Both British and American bomber barons, Air Chief Marshal Sir Arthur Harris and Lt. Gen. Carl Spaatz, believed bombing alone would do for Germany, without the need for an invasion. Eisenhower wanted to use some of the bombers to soften up northern France, destroying roads, bridges and railways, wrecking German chances of sending in reinforcements after the invasion. That idea, and Eisenhower's demand to have overall command of the bombers, led to a head-on confrontation. It was only resolved in his favor when he threatened to resign and Roosevelt backed him.

By early 1944, one million Americans had transformed southern England. Camps blanketed huge areas. Fields, marshalling yards, railheads and ports were crammed with tanks, trucks, armored cars, and planes.

Training intensified. Tank crews became adept at piloting the floating tanks with their "duplex drive" combination of tracks and propellers – DD's, or Donald Ducks, as they were known; glider pilots learned how to crash land in the dark; demolition teams practised on mined obstacles; infantrymen did their inadequate best to prepare for the moment when the ramps went down and they faced waist-deep water and hails of lead. Troops assaulted replicas of German batteries, American Rangers tackled cliffs with the help of fire-brigade ladders. Once, training became part of the war. On the night of April 27–28, a convoy of landing-ships ran into a group of German E-boats, which sank two of the Allied vessels, killing 639 Americans.

With the new rise in troop numbers, the shortage of landing craft again became critical. Another 1,000 were needed. To ensure there would be enough, the date of the invasion was postponed by a month – until June 5. On this day and the two following, conditions would again be right – the moon full for the bombers, the tide low around about dawn for the sea-borne invaders – and there would be more time for training.

But the delay also meant a tougher task, for it gave the Germans more time to harden the Atlantic Wall defences they had been building since 1942. In those two years, blockhouses and gun-emplacements loomed over the coast of continental Europe from Norway to Spain. From Normandy to Calais, work proceeded at a frantic pace, driven forward by Field Marshal Erwin Rommel, appointed in January, 1944, to command Army Group B in north France. He drove his men hard, for he knew that in other respects the

A German observer looks out from his concrete gun emplacement on the Normandy coast

Allied air superiority proved vital during the Normandy landings. Aircraft like the Mosquito were frequently used to attack targets requiring great precision such as radar sites

German forces were in danger, a danger created from their own confused command structure. Rommel commanded two armies (the 7th and 15th). But the seven divisions of tanks which should have been available to him had their own commander, General Leo Geyr von Schweppenburg. Rommel, tank commander par excellence, demanded total control. Hitler compromised, giving Rommel three of the tank divisions, with their own HQ, 47th Panzer Corps, still being established in early June, and setting up the remaining four as a reserve under the control of the Army's Supreme Headquarters (OKW) – which meant under his direct command through 1st SS Panzer Corps based in Rouen. In effect, over half the tanks within reach of Normandy needed Hitler's own orders to respond. This was to prove a decisive flaw on D-Day itself and for the battles that followed.

Rommel was left with only one course of action: to make the Atlantic Wall impregnable, to turn this section of the European coast into a fortress. "The

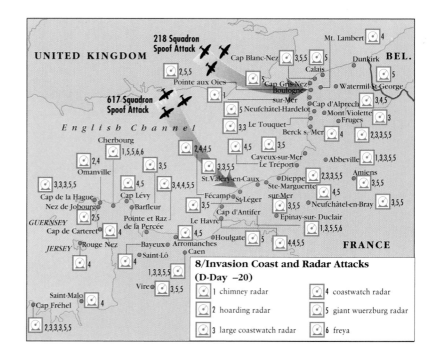

8/Invasion Coast and Radar Attacks (D-Day −20)

1 chimney radar	4 coastwatch radar
2 hoarding radar	5 giant wuerzburg radar
3 large coastwatch radar	6 freya

enemy must be annihilated before he reaches our main battlefield," he ordered. "We must stop him in the water." To do that, he wanted to lay two great belts of mines all along the coast – 200 million of them to turn the beaches into a "zone of death." He knew he had little time left. Throughout the Spring of 1944, he travelled back and forth, driving forward construction remorselessly, until the high water mark was a formidable array of bristling iron and mines, backed by concrete pill-boxes, walls and artillery. In fact, there simply was not enough time, men or material to complete his plans. The coast was too long, the defences too scattered.

To the Allies, however, his achievements meant it would now be impossible to land at night, for the invaders would have to see their way through the maze of obstacles. For the same reason, they could not land at high tide. But the lower the tide, the greater the distance to be covered on foot. There was little choice. The men would have to land on a rising tide, and clear ways through the barriers.

They would be horribly exposed. To help them, Montgomery decided on a tactic never tried before in an amphibious assault: to send in some of Hobart's floating tanks with the troops. Next would come the other specialized tanks to flail paths through the minefields and bridge the walls. With luck, ways inland would then be open.

None of this would be of any use, however, without two other vital advantages: surprise and air superiority.

Air superiority already seemed assured. With the introduction of the American P-51D Mustang fighter, with its 2,300-mile range, in February, 1944, no part of the Reich was safe from the Anglo-American bombers. Flying armadas of 1,000 bombers battered the German heartland almost daily, shattering German industry, cutting aircraft production, inhibiting effective defence and retaliation. In April, her oil supplies were cut by 20 percent. In Normandy, railways, bridges and marshalling yards were pounded by 70,000 tons of bombs, making it increasingly hard for extra troops to sweep into Normandy. Another 200,000 tons of bombs destroyed ammunition dumps,

German Freya Radar of the type used on the Normandy coast. These were sited within protective walls and given anti-aircraft gun protection

camps and depots.

The need for surprise was the second crucial element in Allied strategy. Morgan warned that even 48 hours of advance notice would ruin chances of a successful invasion. With so much at stake, and so many people involved, the task of preserving security was virtually impossible.

The only answer to the possible release of real information was to release a mass of disinformation, a task co-ordinated by an agency named London Controlling Section. Its aim, in a modern analogy, was to create so much noise that the enemy could not sift meaning from nonsense. The agency did this with every means available: double agents, rumor, fake radio messages, fake troops, sabotage. A fictitious Fourth Army, headquartered under Edinburgh Castle, threatened the invasion of Norway so effectively that 27 German divisions remained there instead of moving south.

Another fake army, one million strong, was supposedly gathering in the southeast, prior to an invasion at Calais. Fake landing craft from Shepperton Film Studios littered the River Thames. Fields were clogged with ammunition dumps, field kitchens, guns and planes – all fake. Dover harbor was overshadowed by a huge fake oil dock. The deception acquired a cloak of reality when the fake troops were allocated two real Canadian and American armies, which were in fact gathering for the real Normandy invasion.

It worked. Since few German reconnaissance aircraft now flew over southern England, their information was sparse. Captured documents later showed that the Germans believed the Allies had over twice the actual forces available, and that the blow would probably fall in Calais in July.

In their turn the Allies had the advantage of a huge mass of detailed information about German responses. Frogmen monitored the beaches, reconnaissance planes took pictures, French Resistance agents sent radio reports of troop movements.

Looming over all, however, was the one big unknown – the weather. On that everything depended. There were only three days each month with the

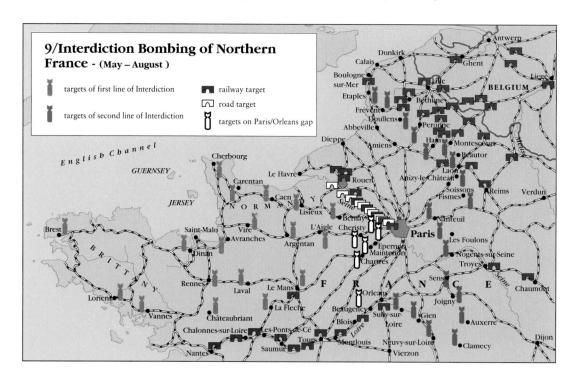

9/Interdiction Bombing of Northern France - (May – August)

targets of first line of Interdiction

targets of second line of Interdiction

railway target

road target

targets on Paris/Orleans gap

right conditions of time, tide and moon-phase. In addition, the wind had to be between critical limits – 12 mph onshore and 18 mph offshore – if the landing craft were to remain stable. Visibility had to be a good three miles so that the ships could bombard accurately. For the bombers, cloud-cover had to be no more than 60 percent, and over 3,000 feet. High winds would scatter the paratroops. Odds against such conditions occurring together were reckoned to be no more than 50 to 1.

Almost certainly, something would go wrong, and there was nothing that anyone could do about it. A delay of a day, perhaps two, might be possible, but to delay another month would be unthinkable. Impossible to contemplate feeding over a million men, keeping them under wraps, and sustaining morale for a month – word would be out in days, the whole operation destroyed. Yet to undo what had been done, without action, would be an equal disaster. In either case, the waste, the loss of morale, the failure to invade, would have catastrophic consequences for the future of the war. Germany would have all the time she needed to rally her defences.

So far so good. Early May was beautiful, all sunshine and gentle breezes. Eisenhower confirmed the date to Stalin, who continued with preparations for a huge Eastern Front offensive to coincide with the palnned advance through Normandy.

The Allies were thus shocked when, in May, Hitler became suddenly convinced that Normandy, not the Pas de Calais, would bear the brunt of the assault. A Panzer division moved to Caen, anti-glider obstacles sprouted in nearby fields, and troops arrived on the Cotentin Peninsula. At a stroke, the opposition – six infantry divisions, two panzer divisions, with another two not far away – looked far more formidable.

Could there have been a security leak? In a famous incident, the Daily Telegraph crossword on May 2 and May 27 contained in its answers three of the operational codenames – the US landing-beaches, Utah and Omaha, and Overlord itself. In the flap that followed, MI5 descended on the bemused

Pre-invasion, the Allied army chiefs confer. General Sir B.L. Montgomery with his two invasion army commanders, Lieut-General M.C. Dempsey commanding the 2nd British Army and Lieut-General O.N. Bradley, commanding the 1st U.S. Army

Field Marshal Erwin Rommel
inspects his troops in
Normandy

compiler, only to conclude it was a bizarre
coincidence. Nor were they able to trace any other
leak. Hitler's moves had been based on the raw
intuition on which he prided himself.

On May 15, with three weeks to go, Eisenhower
and his team of commanders outlined the plan in the
presence of King George VI. The meeting took place
at St Paul's School in Hammersmith, with the King
and the western Allies' most eminent commanders
sitting on school benches. After an introduction by
Eisenhower, Montgomery explained the assault – two
armadas, one for the three British beaches in the east
and one for the American beaches in the west, would
head out of port a day before the attack (D-1), and
gather during the night. They were to be the
vanguard of the 7,000 vessels available for the
invasion as a whole. Soon after midnight, with the
armada approaching the coast, two aerial forces, one
British and the other American, would begin their
parachute and glider drops. By daybreak the flanks of
the 59-mile front would be secure. Then, shortly after
dawn, would come the air and naval bombardment,
followed by the landings by 170,000 men in eight
divisions. It would take a day to secure the beaches.
The next day (D+1) forces would link up, and create

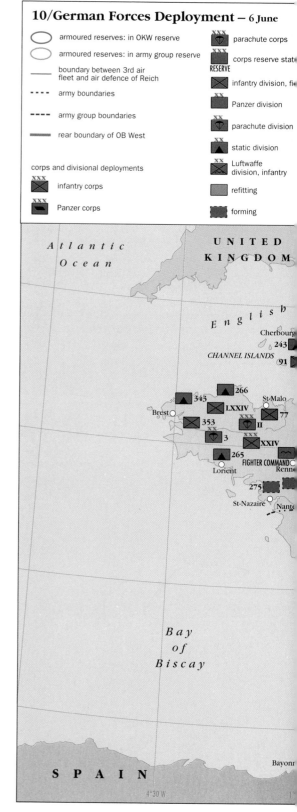

10/German Forces Deployment – 6 June

- armoured reserves: in OKW reserve
- armoured reserves: in army group reserve
- boundary between 3rd air fleet and air defence of Reich
- army boundaries
- army group boundaries
- rear boundary of OB West

corps and divisional deployments
- infantry corps
- Panzer corps

- parachute corps
- corps reserve stati **RESERVE**
- infantry division, fie
- Panzer division
- parachute division
- static division
- Luftwaffe division, infantry
- refitting
- forming

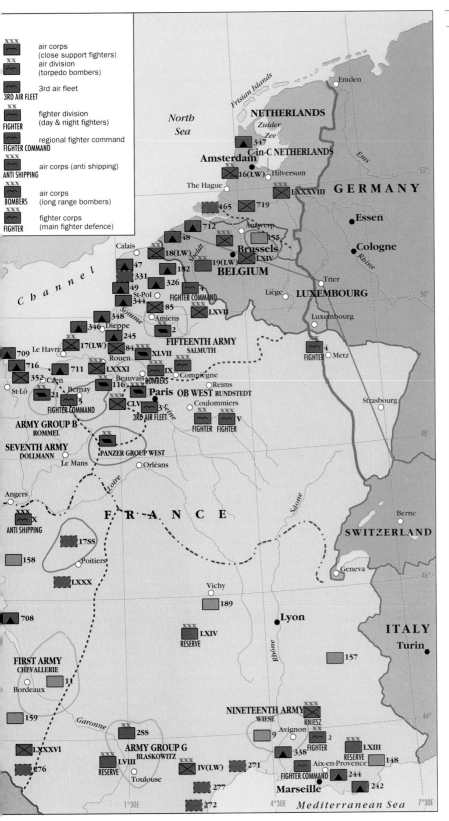

Legend:

- air corps (close support fighters) — **XXX**
- air division (torpedo bombers) — **XX**
- 3rd air fleet — **3RD AIR FLEET**
- fighter division (day & night fighters) — **XX FIGHTER**
- regional fighter command — **FIGHTER COMMAND**
- air corps (anti shipping) — **XXX ANTI SHIPPING**
- air corps (long range bombers) — **XXX BOMBERS**
- fighter corps (main fighter defence) — **XXX FIGHTER**

Map labels:

North Sea · Frisian Islands · Emden · NETHERLANDS · Zuider Zee · 347 · C-in-C NETHERLANDS · Amsterdam · 16(LW) · Hilversum · GERMANY · The Hague · LXXXVIII · 465 · 719 · Essen · 712 · Antwerp · 48 · 155 · Brussels · Cologne · Calais · 18(LW) · 182 · 19(LW) · LXIV · BELGIUM · 47 · 331 · 326 · 4 · Trier · 49 · St-Pol · 344 · 85 · FIGHTER COMMAND · Liège · LUXEMBOURG · 348 · Amiens · LXVII · Luxembourg · 346 · Dieppe · 245 · Somme · 17(LW) · 84 · XLVII · FIFTEENTH ARMY · SALMUTH · 4 · Metz · FIGHTER · 709 · Le Havre · 711 · Rouen · LXXXI · IX · Compiègne · 716 · Beauvais · BOMBERS · 352 · Caen · 116 · Reims · Strasbourg · St-Lô · 21 · Bernay · 5 · Paris · OB WEST · RUNDSTEDT · FIGHTER COMMAND · CLV · Coulommiers · 3rd Corps · 3RD AIR FLEET · ARMY GROUP B · ROMMEL · FIGHTER · FIGHTER · V · SEVENTH ARMY · DOLLMANN · PANZER GROUP WEST · Le Mans · Orléans · Angers · FRANCE · Loire · Saône · Berne · ANTI SHIPPING · SWITZERLAND · 17SS · 158 · Poitiers · Geneva · LXXX · Vichy · 189 · Lyon · ITALY · Turin · LXIV RESERVE · Rhône · 157 · FIRST ARMY · CHEVALLERIE · 11 · Bordeaux · 159 · Garonne · NINETEENTH ARMY · WIESE · KNIESZ · 2SS · Avignon · 9 · ARMY GROUP G · BLASKOWITZ · 338 · FIGHTER · LXIII RESERVE · 148 · 708 · LXXXVI · LVIII RESERVE · IV(LW) · 271 · Aix-en-Provence · 244 · 242 · 276 · Toulouse · FIGHTER COMMAND · 277 · Marseille · 272 · Mediterranean Sea

1°30E · 4°30E · 7°30E

Strength of Occupying Forces in France 1 March 1944

Army	806,927
SS & Police	85,230
Volunteers (foreigners)	61,439
Allies	13,631
Airforce*	337,140
Navy	96,084
Armed Aux. Forces	145,611
TOTAL ARMED FORCES	**1,400,451**

* Airforce figures give a false impression of German air strength in France. Anti-aircraft artillery (flak) was under direct Luftwaffe command. These formations alone accounted for over 100,000 men. As well as their A-A duties, they could be re-deployed as ground formations. Also under Luftwaffe command were just over 30,000 parachute troops.

The approximate number of aircraft available for operations was 890, controlled by the Third Air Fleet, commanded by Field-Marshal Sperrle.

Introduced in 1942, the German Tiger heavy battle tank was one of the most formidable armored fighting vehicles in the world. It was equipped with the famed 88mm KwK 36 gun and 100mm frontal armor that few Allied battlefield weapons of the time could penetrate except at almost point blank range

The 88mm, probably the best gun produced during the war, used in the anti-tank role, it destroyed many Allied tanks. Here used in its original anti-aircraft role

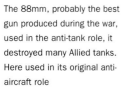

an expanding pocket of newly conquered territory.

This was merely the cutting edge of the axe. Behind would come the weight, the vehicles, men, ammunition, guns, and all their supporting equipment – 13 divisions after a day, 17 by the third day, 21 within two weeks – ready for a break-out eastwards towards Paris, the Rhine and the heartland of the Reich. All would be done beneath an umbrella of some 5,000 bombers and over 5,000 fighter planes. It was a formidable undertaking – the equivalent, as one supply officer put it, of shifting a city the size of Birmingham over the Channel and then keeping it on the move – but now, at last, everything seemed in place.

The weather held. At the end of May, the troops, broken down into boat-load units, were sealed up behind barbed wire, with little to do but wait. In final briefings, the infantry were shown exactly what would confront them, though they still did not know where exactly they were going. Air crews saw their landing areas on a film of the model of the area, projected through a blue filter to simulate moonlight. In mile after square mile of camps, the Americans in Devon and Dorset, the British in Hampshire and Sussex, a great silence fell. All British military mail was censored, and American troops could no longer contact the States. In London, even diplomatic mail was censored. A small contingent of war correspondents vanished, absorbed into the units with which they would travel.

On May 29, on the basis of a guarded long-range weather forecast, the whole vast machine began to grind into motion. Warships and tugs towing Mulberries headed south, men marched to the waiting ships. The crowds who watched, waved and wept did not know where the men were going, any more than the men knew themselves, but everyone knew something huge was happening, that this was the opening of the Second Front. By June 3, the invaders were aboard.

That evening, though, everything changed. In the Portsmouth mansion that served as SHAEF's advance command post, the Allied commanders had to grapple with their worst fears. The weather was closing in. The head of the meteorological team, Group-Captain James Stagg, faced with providing what one historian has termed as "probably the most important weather prediction in history," reported that the outlook was "disturbed and complex." Three depressions straddled the Atlantic, heading for the Channel, bringing high winds and low cloud, the worst summer weather for decades. If things were as bad as predicted, there could be no assault by sea or land.

Eisenhower decided to postpone a decision until the dawn.

At 4.15 a.m, the commanders met again, drawn with tension. It was a still and cloudless Sunday morning, perfect invasion weather. But far to the west, in the churning Atlantic depressions, nothing had changed.

Eisenhower postponed D-Day by one day.

In mid-morning, the storm struck the Irish Sea, and moved steadily eastwards. Warships turned, and drove their way back to port. All over southern England, in ports and inlets, landing craft bobbed on surging waves, and the men locked in their ships turned pasty-faced with seasickness.

That evening, with the wind and rain battering at the windows, the commanders gathered in the library of Southwick House. This was the moment of final decision. There could not be a postponement long enough to wait out the storm, for that would mean reversing the avalanche of men and material pouring into the camps left empty by the invading troops, risking security, even threatening the success of the Russian summer offensive.

Stagg, though, offered the startling possibility of a reprieve. The storm trailed in its wake a cold front, which was moving faster and further south than expected. Starting the following afternoon, there was likely to be an improvement; though only for 24 hours. The dangers of invading during so brief an opportunity were obvious: even if the invasion force landed successfully, the back-up forces might not be able to. An army of 170,000 might be stranded in Normandy, caught in a tightening enemy noose.

Consulting his subordinates, Eisenhower finally turned to Montgomery. "Do you see any reason why we shouldn't go on Tuesday?" he asked.

"No," Montgomery replied. "I would say 'Go'."

At 9.45, Eisenhower told his commanders: "I don't see how we can possibly do anything else. I am quite positive we must give the order."

There was one more meeting, early on Monday, June 5. The wind still whipped rain across gray skies, but Stagg held firm: "As I see it, the little that has changed is in the direction of optimism."

Eisenhower's face, taut with tension, relaxed into the famous, broad smile. "OK," he said, "we'll go."

The Panzer Mk.V (Panther) armed with 75mm Kwk 42 gun. This very high velocity weapon could penetrate the armor of any Allied tank with ease. Slow turret traverse was almost its only weakness

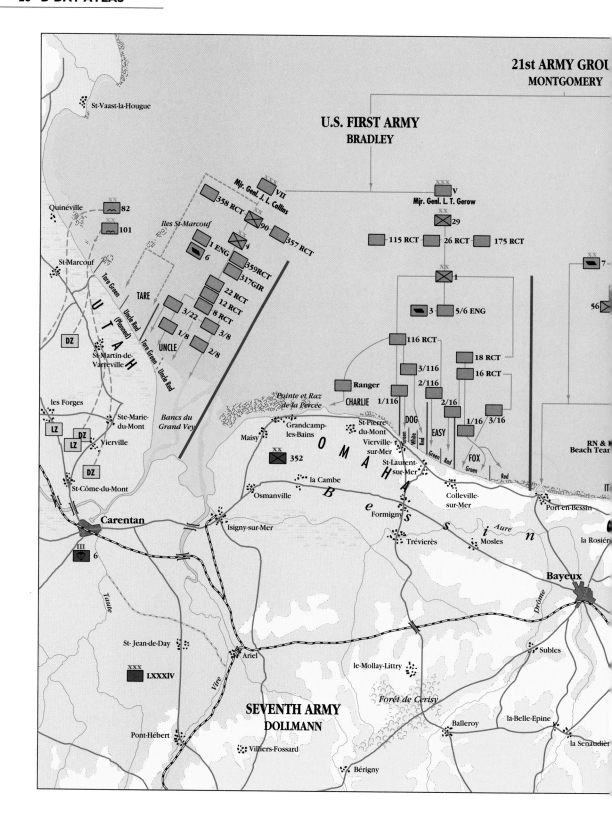

21st ARMY GROU
MONTGOMERY

U.S. FIRST ARMY
BRADLEY

St-Vaast-la-Hougue

Quinéville — 82
— 101

VII
Mjr. Genl. J. L. Collins

Iles St-Marcouf

358 RCT
90
357 RCT

St-Marcouf

1 ENG
4
6
359 RCT
317 GIR

les Forges

Tare Green
Uncle Red
(Planned)
Tare Green / Uncle Red

TARE

UTAH

22 RCT
12 RCT
8 RCT

3/22
1/8
UNCLE
2/8
3/8

DZ

St-Martin-de-
Varreville

Ste-Marie-
du-Mont

LZ
DZ
LZ

Vierville

DZ

St-Côme-du-Mont

Bancs du
Grand Vey

Pointe et Raz
de la Percée

Ranger

CHARLIE

1/116

Grandcamp-
les-Bains

Maisy

352

la Cambe

Osmanville

Isigny-sur-Mer

O
M
A
H
A
S

B
e
s

St-Pierre-
du-Mont

Vierville-
sur-Mer

DOG

Green
White
Red

Green
Red

EASY

Green
Red

FOX

Red

116 RCT

3/116
2/116

2/16

1/16 3/16

St-Laurent-
sur-Mer

Colleville-
sur-Mer

Formigny

Trévières

Mosles

Aure

Bayeux

V
Mjr. Genl. L. T. Gerow

29

115 RCT 26 RCT 175 RCT

1

3 5/6 ENG

18 RCT
16 RCT

7

56

RN &
Beach Tear

IT

Port-en-Bessin

la Rosiér

Drôme

Carentan

III
6

Taute

St-Jean-de-Day

LXXXIV

Pont-Hébert

Villiers-Fossard

Vire

Ariel

le-Mollay-Littry

Forêt de Cerisy

SEVENTH ARMY
DOLLMANN

Bérigny

Subles

Balleroy

la-Belle-Epine

la Senaudier

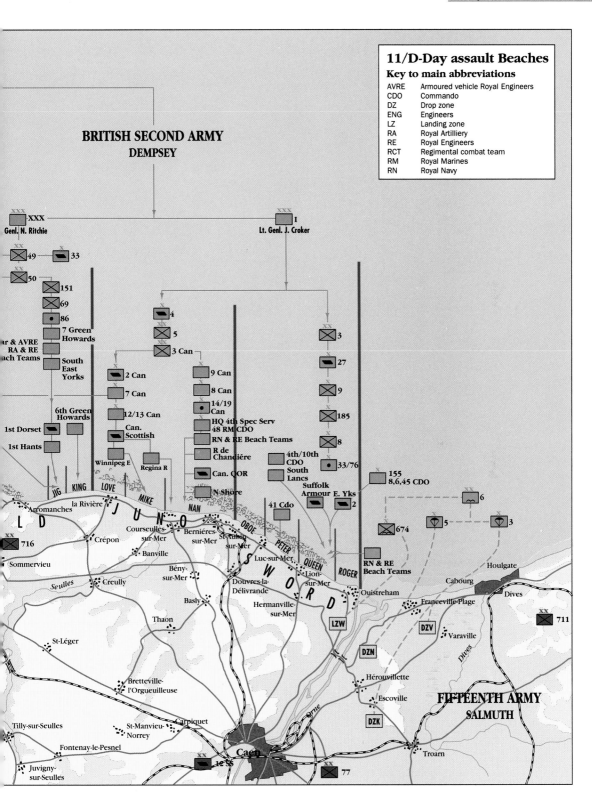

11/D-Day assault Beaches
Key to main abbreviations

AVRE	Armoured vehicle Royal Engineers
CDO	Commando
DZ	Drop zone
ENG	Engineers
LZ	Landing zone
RA	Royal Artillery
RE	Royal Engineers
RCT	Regimental combat team
RM	Royal Marines
RN	Royal Navy

BRITISH SECOND ARMY
DEMPSEY

XXX
Genl. N. Ritchie

XXX
I
Lt. Genl. J. Croker

49

33

50

151

69

86

7 Green
Howards

ar & AVRE
RA & RE
ach Teams

South
East
Yorks

6th Green
Howards

1st Dorset

1st Hants

Winnipeg E

Regina R

4

5

3 Can

2 Can

7 Can

12/13 Can

Can.
Scottish

9 Can

8 Can

14/19
Can

HQ 4th Spec Serv
48 RM CDO

RN & RE Beach Teams

R de
Chandiére

Can. QOR

N Shore

41 Cdo

3

27

9

185

8

33/76

4th/10th
CDO
South
Lancs

Suffolk
Armour E. Yks

155
8,6,45 CDO

674

6

5

3

RN & RE
Beach Teams

Houlgate

Cabourg

Dives

Franceville-Plage

716

Arromanches

la Rivière

Crépon

Sommervieu

Seulles

Creully

Banville

Bény-
sur-Mer

Courseulles-
sur-Mer

Berniéres-
sur-Mer

St-Aubin
sur-Mer

Luc-sur-Mer

Lion-
sur-Mer

Ouistreham

JIG KING LOVE JUNO MIKE NAN OBOE PETER QUEEN ROGER

LD D SWORD

Basly

Thaon

St-Léger

Bretteville-
l'Orgueuilleuse

Tilly-sur-Seulles

Fontenay-le-Pesnel

Juvigny-
sur-Seulles

St-Manvieu-
Norrey

Carpiquet

Caen

12 SS

77

Douvres-la-
Délivrande

Hermanville-
sur-Mer

LZW

DZN

Hérouvillette

Escoville

DZK

Orne

Troarn

Dives

Varaville

DZV

711

FIFTEENTH ARMY
SALMUTH

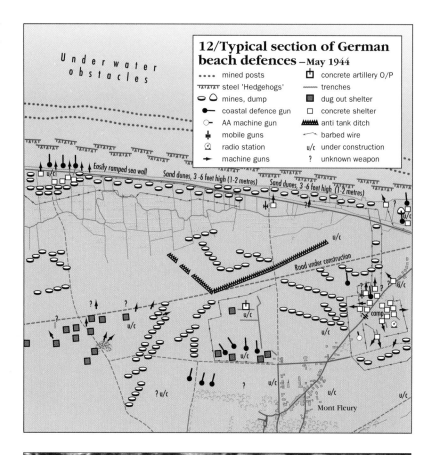

12/Typical section of German beach defences – May 1944

Underwater obstacles

••••	mined posts	⌂	concrete artillery O/P
ᴛᴀᴛᴀᴛᴀᴛ	steel 'Hedgehogs'	——	trenches
◯◠	mines, dump	◼	dug out shelter
●—	coastal defence gun	☐	concrete shelter
◯—	AA machine gun	▲▲▲▲	anti tank ditch
⊢	mobile guns	⌒	barbed wire
⊘	radio station	u/c	under construction
→	machine guns	?	unknown weapon

Easily ramped sea wall

Sand dunes, 3 -6 feet high (1-2 metres)

Sand dunes, 3 -6 feet high (1-2 metres)

Road under construction

camp

Mont Fleury

The German "Atlantic Wall" consisted of some 2,400 miles of beach defences including tank obstacles like these "Dragon's teeth"

2 ASSAULT FROM THE AIR

Early on June 5, nearly 5,000 Allied ships put out into blustery seas. Mine-sweepers cleared 10 lanes through the German minefields, leading the way for battleships, cruisers, frigates, landing craft for men, landing craft for tanks, ships to repair machines, hospital ships, ammunition ships, ships whose sole purpose was to be sunk to create breakwaters. Protected at sea and in the air from German attack, they settled into position off the French coast soon after an early stormy dusk.

Meanwhile, in England, the last to leave would be the first into battle. They were the 24,000 paratroopers and glider-borne troops of the British 6th Airborne Divison and the U.S. 82nd and 101st Airborne Divisions. As night fell, the men were driven to 22 airfields where the 1,200 transport planes and 700 gliders awaited them. The greatest amphibious assault ever was about to be preceded by the greatest airborne assault to date.

Between sunset and midnight, the men, their faces blackened, climbed aboard, each of them weighed down by 85–100 pounds of gear for fighting, for survival, for specialized tasks. A U.S. pathfinder in the 82nd carried a chute, a reserve chute, fragmentation grenades, gammon bombs, a phosphorus grenade, rations, fighting knife, waterbottle, an anti-tank mine, rifle, pistol, morphia capsule and a forces issue of *Oliver Twist*. Engines roared, and the sky filled with dark shadows, winking red-and-green navigation lights, and the rumble of engines. Below, in the blacked-out towns and villages, there were few awake to watch but those who did would never forget the sight and sound of that immense armada.

In the leading British planes, due to arrive over the Caen area around midnight, were the pathfinders, parachutists carrying the lights and radar-beacons that would mark the landing zones for the paratroopers and gliders. Behind came six planes towing a glider each, carrying five platoons of the 2nd Battalion Oxfordshire and Buckinghamshire Light Infantry – the "Ox and Bucks" – and a company of Royal Engineers. A gusty wind flipped the gliders back and forth, up and down, at the end of their ropes. Now and then, gaps in the rain-clouds revealed the full moon above, and below the ships, numerous as fish, dark oblongs cutting white moon-flecked wakes.

By then, the first blows of Operation Overlord had already been struck – by the French Resistance who had a vital role to play. Working in collaboration with the British Special Operations Executive, they had developed scores of sabotage operations to destroy rail-links and communication lines. They had been ready for five days now, alerted to the imminence of the invasion by the BBC's French service quoting – along with a mass of other enigmatic phrases, some coded instructions, some meaningless – the first three lines from Paul Verlaine's poem "Autumn Song":

> *Les sanglots longs*
> *Des violons*
>   *De l'automne ...*
> (The drawn-out sobs of the violins of autumn.)

Then, on the evening of June 5, while the paratroopers prepared to board, came the second half of the six-line verse, the sign that invasion would come within 48 hours:

> *Blessent mon coeur*
> *D'une langueur*
>   *Monotone.*
> (Wound my heart with a monotonous languor.)

German beach defences photographed by low-level Allied reconnaissance aircraft to identify specific types of obstacles on each of the invasion beaches

The Resistance movement played a vital role on the success of the D-Day landings. Here a Resistance Fighter checks out a house that was once a German HQ

It was time to start the sabotage operations. That night, the Resistance carried out more than 1,000 attacks.

By some efficient espionage, the German High Command had actually been given both the code and the news of its broadcast by a double agent. Astonishingly, the information was ignored. The Commander-in-Chief West, Field Marshal Gerd von Rundstedt simply did not take the information seriously. There had been so many false alarms. The weather was bad, and the Allies would surely not be so foolish as to broadcast news of the invasion on the BBC. In brief, the blitz of fake information had worked: the Germans could no longer tell truth from deception.

If the coming air drops and bombing raids were not to give the game away, the Germans also had to be convinced that the real assault would take place elsewhere. Bombers began dropping dummy paratroopers all over Normandy, radio transmitters jammed German radar stations, other bombers attacked targets around the Pas de Calais, fake German broadcasts ordered Luftwaffe planes to defend Calais, and the French Resistance began destroying German communications centres.

In the Channel, heading towards Calais, came an ingenious electronic mirage. Two dozen motor launches towed 29-foot high balloons carrying reflectors that mimicked the radar images of 10,000-ton troop transporters. Above, RAF bombers circled, dropping strips of aluminium foil – Window, as it was called – that reflected radar echoes like those of planes. Those radar stations still operating reported the imminent arrival of a huge air and sea force. With Luftwaffe fighters on their way to oppose the non-existent enemy, the skies over Normandy were clear for the Allied bombers, paratroopers and gliders.

In the darkness ahead, around midnight (11.00 p.m. in France and Germany) the Germans settled down to a quiet if stormy night, suspecting nothing. In view of the bad weather, Admiral Theodor Krancke, the west's naval commander, had cancelled the usual torpedo-boat patrols. General Friedrich Dollmann, commander of the Seventh Army, convinced the

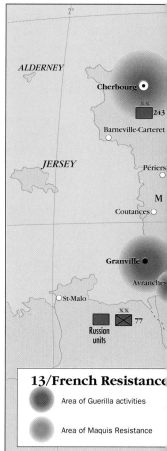

13/French Resistance

Area of Guerilla activities

Area of Maquis Resistance

invasion would not happen for another month, had told his senior officers to attend war games in Rennes, 125 miles inland, to study (of all things) an Allied invasion of Normandy. At the HQ of 84th Corps in St-Lô, staff were arranging a stiff little birthday celebration for their commander, General Erich Marcks, an austere man who had lost a leg in Russia. At the HQ of Army Group B, all was quiet. Rommel had left for his home in Herrlingen, near Ulm, on the Danube for his wife Lucie-Maria's birthday, before driving on to see Hitler in Berchtesgaden. Rundstedt was asleep in Saint-Germain.

Over the Channel, just after midnight, the first wave of British airborne invaders – 200 men in six gliders towed by Albemarles – could see through cloud-gaps glimpses of the sands of France and the parallel ribbons of two waterways, the River Orne and the Caen Canal, leading south through Caen itself. Just two miles inland, between Caen and the sea, were their targets: the two bridges near Benouville that carried the main coast road over the waterways. The bridges were wired for demolition.

The two bridges and other targets – a battery at Merville, five bridges over the Dives, high ground between the two rivers – had to be seized to secure the east flank of the invasion front to stop German tanks of the 21st Panzers in Caen charging in from the east and crushing Overlord before the troops got off the beaches.

With the attention of the German gunners taken by the bombers, the pathfinder paratroopers leaped unseen, and the glider pilots released their

A French Resistance Fighter, complete with captured German rifle. Women often played a vital and active role in Resistance activities

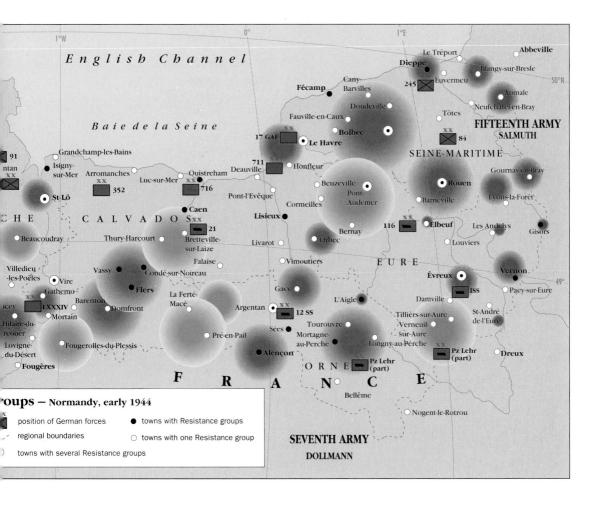

…oups — Normandy, early 1944

- position of German forces
- regional boundaries
- towns with several Resistance groups
- ● towns with Resistance groups
- ○ towns with one Resistance group

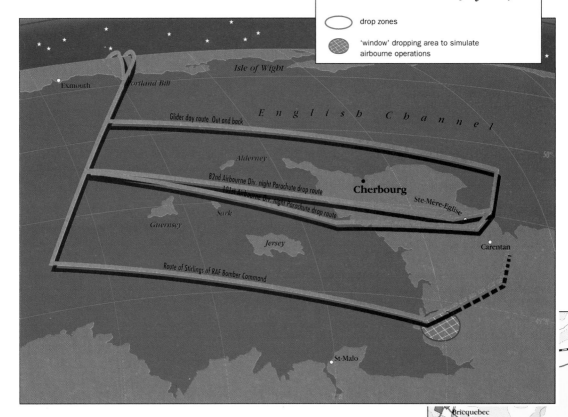

drop zones

'window' dropping area to simulate airborne operations

Isle of Wight

Exmouth Portland Bill

E n g l i s h   C h a n n e l

Glider day route Out and back

Alderney

82nd Airbourne Div. night Parachute drop route

101st Airbourne Div. night Parachute drop route

Cherbourg

Ste-Mère-Eglise

Sark

Guernsey

Jersey

Carentan

Route of Stirlings of RAF Bomber Command

St-Malo

tow-ropes to begin the silent descent through the cloud and rain. Then, a shouted order, and the rattle and rustle of equipment as the pilots swung their gliders for the final approach.

They were on target. The first glider, after hitting a cow, careered to a stop with its splintered nose in a barbed wire fence just 50 yards from the Caen Canal swingbridge, codenamed Pegasus. Two others ran to a halt yards from the first. The soldiers moved so fast that the Germans on guard, stupefied by the bombing, hardly had time to respond. A machine gun stuttered from a pillbox killing the leading British officer, then was silenced by a grenade through the gunport. Across the bridge, the defenders leaped into their trenches; but by then, the British were running across. The defenders fled. The bridge, its charges defused, was in British hands 10 minutes after landing. By the time the three other gliders reached the river bridge, it was completely undefended.

Meanwhile, pathfinders had marked zones for the second wave of the 6th Airborne, two brigades 2,000 strong. At 12.50 a.m. they made their drop near Ranville, a mile east of the two bridges. Scattered by the wind, they were pulled together on the ground by a hunting-horn. Then, while one battalion went to reinforce their colleagues at the bridges, another settled down to secure the approach road from the east. A third battalion cleared a landing zone of anti-glider poles for the next glider-borne wave, which would arrive two hours later to set up the divisional headquarters with anti-tank guns, machine guns and jeeps. They went on to drive German infantry from Ranville, the first French village to be liberated.

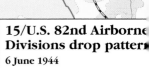

Bricquebec

Douve

15/U.S. 82nd Airborne Divisions drop pattern
6 June 1944

Ⓝ planned 82nd drop zone

Ⓓ planned 101st drop zone

actual landings (each dot represents one plane load):

▪ drop zone 'T' units: 507th Parachute infantry

▲ drop zone 'O' units: 505th parachute infantry, Div HQ and 6 loads of support troops

• drop zone 'N' units: 508th parachute infantry and 15 loads of support troops

▪▲• 101st landing

11 miles

▲ distance and direction of landing
▪▪▪▪ beyond the map limit

La-Haye-du-Puits

Further east, on the Dives, the 6th Airborne's 3rd Brigade got off to a bad start. Their task was to blow up the five bridges over the Dives and take the high ground on the Caen side. Some of the landing zones had been wrongly marked. Some of the pilots mistook the Orne for the Dives, others veered off course to avoid anti-aircraft fire. Many paras landed miles away, taking days to rejoin their units.

Those who could do so linked up, and rapidly blew up four of the Dives bridges. One group of nine, finding themselves five miles from their target – the last of the bridges at Troarn – commandeered a jeep, roared into Troarn under fire, blew up the bridge, and escaped on foot.

The paras' final mission, given to 9th Battalion, was to take the battery at Merville. Intelligence had described it as a concrete blockhouse protecting four 150-mm guns, defended by a minefield, a 15-foot deep barbed-wire fence, an anti-tank ditch, and something over 130 men in machine-gun nests. The planned assault, rehearsed nine times using a replica built near Newbury, was dramatic: a pre-assault bombing raid by 100 Lancasters, a crash-landing on the site by three gliders, the assault itself from paras, and as a final insurance if the attack failed, a bombardment from the sea.

Almost everything went wrong. The Lancasters missed, hitting a nearby village and a herd of cows. Five gliders carrying the anti-tank guns all broke their tow-ropes and crashed into the sea. And in the jump itself, the pilots veered violently to avoid flak, and the 555 paras landed widely scattered over

A member of the U.S. 82nd Airborne Division, shortly to be dropped inland from Utah Beach concentrating in the area around Ste-Mère-Eglise

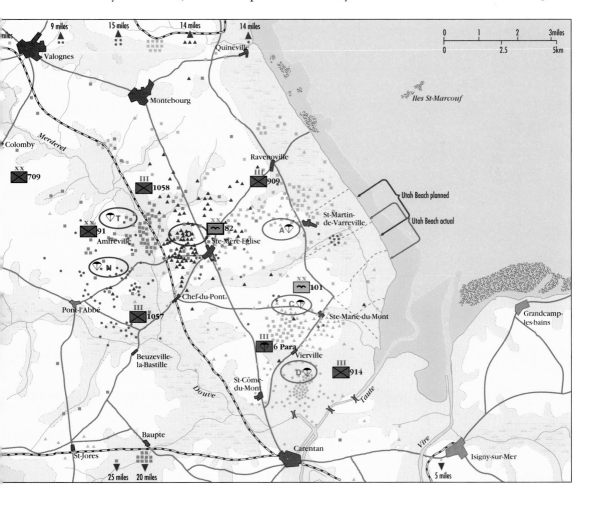

The tightly-packed interior of an American Waco glider

50 square miles of territory. Some fell in swamps on the Dives, where many drowned. The battalion commander, 29-year-old Lt. Col. Terence Otway, managed to assemble a mere 150 men. Their average age was 21, and none had been in battle before. All the heavy equipment – mortars, anti-tank guns, jeeps, mine detectors – was lost. Otway had just one machine-gun, and not much explosive.

Finally, when he got near the battery with his depleted force, only two of the attack gliders appeared (the third had broken its tow-rope on take-off). Pathfinders had already marked a way through the minefield, but Otway's men had no flares to indicate they were ready. One glider banked, and landed four miles away. The other was downed by flak.

Otway gave orders to attack anyway, in two groups. One group took on the machine-gunners hand-to-hand, the other headed for the battery itself, ducking in and out of bomb craters until they were close enough to pour fire in through the doors. The defenders surrendered. In something of an anti-climax, the paras then discovered that the guns were half the size reported, hardly big enough to harry the beaches. They blew them up.

At the cost of the lives of almost half the attackers, the eastern flank of the Overlord assault area was secure. Otway fired a signal flare to inform the ships. A signals officer, preserving radio silence, pulled a carrier-pigeon from his battle-dress, and news of the success flew back across the Channel.

By then, on schedule, 72 gliders bearing the 5th Parachute Brigade had

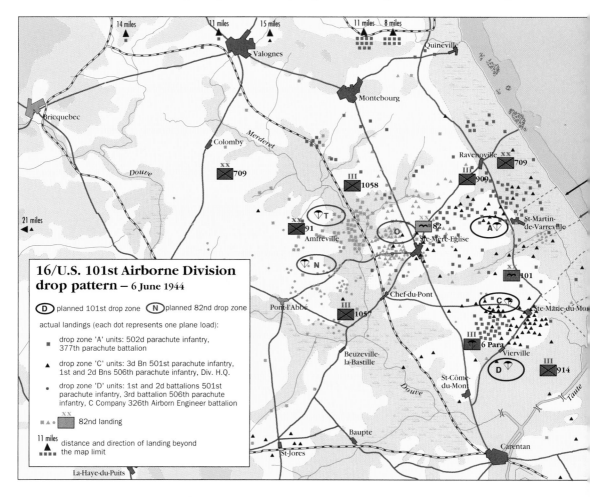

16/U.S. 101st Airborne Division drop pattern – 6 June 1944

(D) planned 101st drop zone (N) planned 82nd drop zone

actual landings (each dot represents one plane load):

- ■ drop zone 'A' units: 502d parachute infantry, 377th parachute battalion

- ▲ drop zone 'C' units: 3d Bn 501st parachute infantry, 1st and 2d Bns 506th parachute infantry, Div. H.Q.

- • drop zone 'D' units: 1st and 2d battalions 501st parachute infantry, 3rd battalion 506th parachute infantry, C Company 326th Airborn Engineer battalion

■ ▲ • ▨ 82nd landing

11 miles ▲ distance and direction of landing beyond the map limit

Paratrooper Private Elmer
Habbs, of Delaware, relaxes
after the capture of Ste-Mère-
Eglise and link-up with the
4th Infantry Division moving
inland from Utah Beach

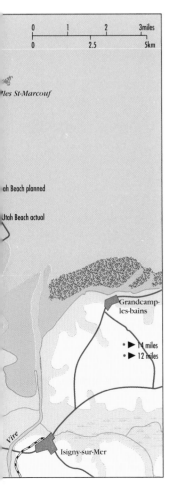

already swung in over the Ranville landing zone, a ploughed field. Twenty-three of them went astray – two collided, one tore through a cottage, others crashed into anti-glider poles – but 49 landed safely. The men linked up, calling half their password, "V for …", listening for the reply, "… Victory!" They rescued several jeeps and 10 anti-tank guns, and worked their way towards their rendezvous, the village's Norman church, where the 6th Airborne's commander, Major General Richard Gale, formed them up. Commandeering a fine chestnut horse found grazing nearby, he marched his men off to the chateau he had chosen as his headquarters. There, they fortified the place before the 21st Panzers could counterattack.

Meanwhile, the American airborne forces had started their attack to secure the hinterland of Utah Beach – the western flank of the Overlord assault – and spread inland across the Cotentin Peninsula. It was a tough, possibly suicidal assignment (Air Vice Marshal Trafford Leigh-Mallory had warned Eisenhower to expect 80 percent casualties.) Behind Utah lay a lagoon almost 10 miles long and a mile wide. It was crossed by four causeways. Ten miles inland, the valleys of the Merderet and Douve rivers had been flooded. Only two main roads led inland, across two bridges. It was vital to take the causeways and bridges if the troops due to arrive at dawn were to head inland away from the beach and the coastal strip.

At a quarter past midnight, pathfinders marked four drop zones and a landing zone for gliders. Then, an hour later, some 800 planes, in formations of nine, each screened by fighters, droned over the coast bearing the 13,000 men of the 82nd and 101st Airborne Divisions. General Matthew Ridgway, in command of the 82nd, later recalled how the men, so cumbersome in their armor of gear that they were unable to fit through the toilet door, released their tension by teasing anyone who had to use the toilet bucket.

It was the task of the 101st to take the causeways, the 82nd to take the inland bridges. They needed to land with great precision, within two or three miles of their targets. From the start, there was no precision. The planes had come through cloud, and many were already scattered, flying too high, or too fast, or too far off course even to see the dropzones. As flak whipped up into the night sky, many nervous pilots banked this way and that, forcing the paratroopers to jump blind.

The result was near catastrophe. Some 75 percent of the 13,000 paras dropped so wide of their target areas that they never took any part in the attack. They found themselves lost among fields, hedgerows and lanes, forming small aimless groups, wandering for days from village to village, farm to farm, skirmishing occasionally with German patrols. By good luck, however, the chaos helped. The confused paras inadvertently sowed equal confusion among the Germans, who had no idea what the targets were, where the enemy was, or how many there were.

The 101st – the first to go at 1.30 a.m. – landed over a huge oblong, 25 miles by 15, wide enough to overlap the 82nd. On landing, its commander, Major General Maxwell Taylor, found he had an entire field to himself. It took him half an hour of wandering in the dark to find anyone else – a private. Major General and private embraced in sheer relief.

Slowly, isolated men came together, recognizing each other by the click-click of specially issued metal "crickets," toys like those found in Christmas crackers. They made a sharp noise, easily recognized and, as it turned out, dangerous too. The Germans soon discovered the ruse, and lured many paras to sudden death with captured crickets. That night, Taylor pulled together no more than 1,000 men, only one-sixth of his force, but large enough to secure and hold the western exits of all the causeways.

There were some remarkable individual acts of courage that night. Perhaps the most extraordinary occurred in les Mézières, where Staff Sergeant Harrison Summers turned himself into a one-man army. He and a small group of paras came across a row of houses used as barracks. Told to wipe out the position, he rounded up 15 men. He knew none of them, and they were not enthusiastic. So he attacked alone, kicking open the door of the first house, firing his sub-machine gun at the Germans inside. He killed four; the rest fled. He went on from house to house, backed by his reluctant detachment, and eventually partnered by a private, John Camien. The final house was a mess hall where 15 Germans were eating breakfast. Summers killed them all. Within a few minutes, he had personally shot over 50 men.

Some five miles west, the 82nd Airborne were in even worse trouble than the 101st. The area was strongly defended by the 91st Infantry Division. Two of the three regiments were supposed to blow up the Douve bridges and set up a line of defence along the Merderet, but the flooding of the two rivers was worse than predicted. Areas that looked like huge solid fields in reconnaissance photographs were in fact shallow lakes disguised by long grass. The only solid ground was provided by the raised Cherbourg–Caen railway line. Glider-borne artillery sank. Many men drowned, weighed down by their packs. Many more had no idea where to go. By the time some hauled themselves on to the railway, it was too late to fulfill their mission.

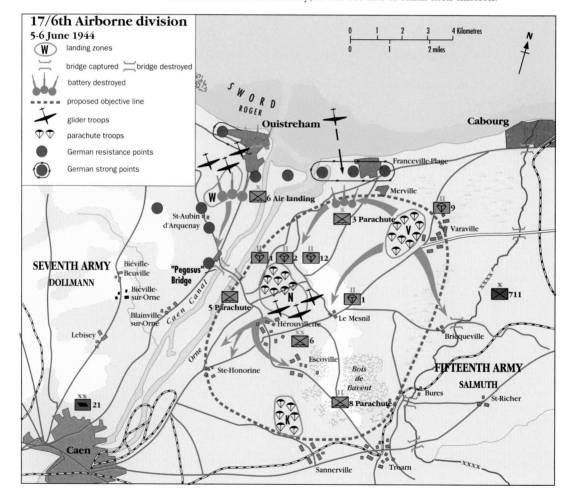

17/6th Airborne division
5-6 June 1944

The main objective, however, was the village of Ste-Mère-Eglise which was to become the key to a north–south defence line along the road leading round towards Omaha Beach. At first, the attack – by the 82nd's 505th Parachute Infantry Regiment – looked like a disaster. Some 30 men fell actually on the village, about 20 of them right in the central square. The German garrison of 100 rushed to the attack. Within a few minutes, in a vicious burst of fighting, all had either been killed or taken prisoner. Private John Steele landed on the church. His parachute caught on the steeple, where he dangled for two and a half hours, playing dead until he was finally taken prisoner. (A dummy parachutist now dangles from the steeple as a tourist attraction.)

To the Germans, it seemed an easy victory. In fact, the fight had hardly started. Most of the 505th had landed as planned in a tight-knit bunch outside the village. The attack, undertaken by 108 men of the 3rd Battalion, quickly drove the Germans out by dawn.

Still, as night gave way to day, there was no co-ordinated German response. Partly, this was a tribute to Allied strategy.

Bombers had knocked out 74 of the 92 radar stations on the Normandy coast. The fake naval and aerial armadas being towed across the Channel towards the Pas de Calais seemed far more convincing than the real force. The few true reports could easily be dismissed as hysterical, or just plain wrong. Dummy parachutists dropping all over Normandy led commanders to ignore real drops. Everywhere, telephone lines had been cut by the Resistance. To the generals nothing was clear.

Even when clarity might have dawned, prejudice and incompetence in the high command crushed initiative. The first senior German officer to realize something important was happening was General Erich Marcks. Shortly after his birthday toast, two reports came through of the airdrops in the Orne estuary and the Cotentin Peninsula. Marcks at once put his own corps and 352nd Infantry Division west of Bayeux on alert, recalled those senior officers heading for the war-games in Rennes and reported up the ladder of command to Seventh Army. General Pemsel, Seventh Army chief-of-staff, called Rommel's chief-of-staff, General Hans Speidel. Speidel passed on the news to Rundstedt. At first Rundstedt was blasé. His staff advised: "C-in-C does not consider this to be a major operation." He soon changed his mind, and decided to order up two more tank divisions, the 12th SS Hitler Youth and Lehr divisions. But that order needed confirmation from Supreme Headquarters – from Hitler himself, in Berchtesgaden. Hitler, however, refused to commit his tanks prematurely, and went to bed with a sleeping draught. For hours, no one did anything of significance at all. In Caen, the 21st Panzers were ready to roll at 2.00 a.m. but no one gave the order. The one man who might have responded effectively, Rommel, was asleep 500 miles away, in his home in Herrlingen.

Historians like to speculate how the invasion would have turned out, if the German high command had been sharper, if Hitler had responded to Rundstedt's request, if the chain of command had not been paralyzed

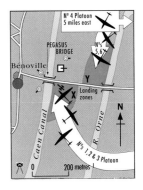

The planned landing zones of the Horsa gliders within yards of the River Orne

A Horsa glider, piloted by Staff Sergeant Wallwork, carrying John Howard and No. 1 Platoon, lying 50 yards from the Caen Canal bridge

by Hitler's self-destructive paranoia. Probably (it is generally agreed), the Allies would have won anyway. But it would have been a lot tougher.

As things were, by early morning it was already too late. The main batteries were silenced, key villages taken, major roads secured, important bridges blown. The noise of battle died.

Then with the dawn came the first boom and rumble of Allied guns opening the bombardment of the coastal defences. All along the coast, explosions sent up gouts of sand, earth and concrete. At a German strongpoint above Utah, Second Lt. Arthur Jahnke stared through his telescope. He saw gray shadows, from horizon to horizon.

The invasion was about to start.

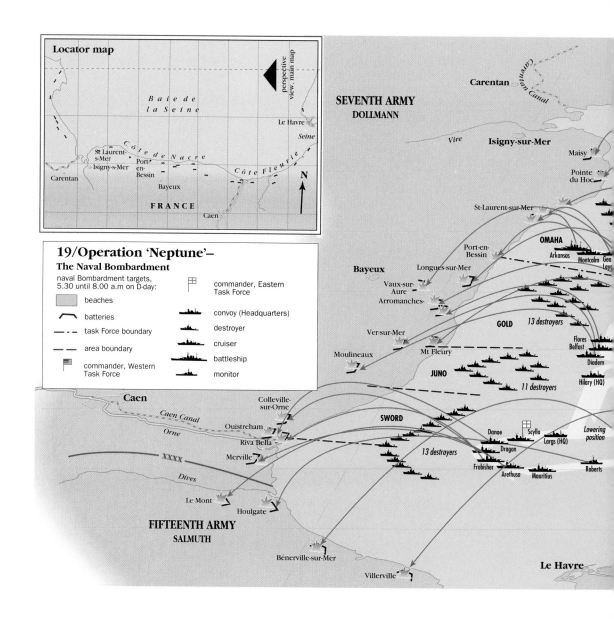

Locator map

*Baie de
la Seine*

Le Havre

Seine

St Laurent-s-Mer
Port-
en-
Bessin

Côte de Nacre

Côte Fleurie

Isigny-s-Mer

Carentan

Bayeux

Caen

FRANCE

N

perspective
view, main map

19/Operation 'Neptune'–

The Naval Bombardment

naval Bombardment targets,
5.30 until 8.00 a.m on D-day:

beaches

batteries

task Force boundary

area boundary

commander, Western
Task Force

commander, Eastern
Task Force

convoy (Headquarters)

destroyer

cruiser

battleship

monitor

SEVENTH ARMY
DOLLMANN

Carentan

Carentan Canal

Vire   Isigny-sur-Mer

Maisy

Pointe
du Hoc

St-Laurent-sur-Mer

Port-en-
Bessin

OMAHA

Arkansas   Montcalm   Geo
Leyg

Bayeux   Longues-sur-Mer

Vaux-sur-
Aure

Arromanches

GOLD   *13 destroyers*

Flores
Belfast

Diadem

Ver-sur-Mer

Moulineaux   Mt Fleury

Hilary (HQ)

JUNO   *11 destroyers*

Caen

Colleville-
sur-Orne

Caen Canal

Ouistreham

Orne

Riva Bella

Merville

SWORD

13 destroyers

Danae   Scylla

Largs (HQ)

Lowering
position

Dragon

Frobisher

Arethusa   Mauritius

Roberts

XXXX

Dives

Le Mont

Houlgate

FIFTEENTH ARMY
SALMUTH

Bénerville-sur-Mer

Villerville

Le Havre

A rocket-equipped assault
craft fires a salvo at the
German defences

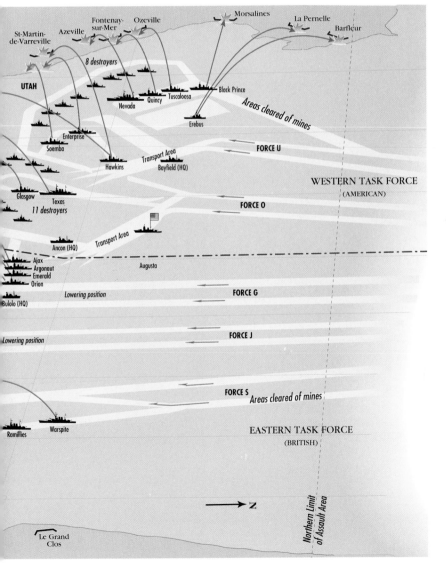

St-Martin-
de-Varreville
Azeville
Fontenay-
sur-Mer Ozeville
Morsalines
La Pernelle
Barfleur
UTAH
8 destroyers
Black Prince
Quincy Tuscaloosa
Nevada
Areas cleared of mines
Erebus
Enterprise
Soemba
FORCE U
Hawkins
Transport Area
Bayfield (HQ)
WESTERN TASK FORCE
(AMERICAN)
Glasgow
Texas
11 destroyers
FORCE O
Transport Area
Ancon (HQ)
Ajax
Argonaut
Emerald
Orion
Augusta
Bulolo (HQ)
Lowering position
FORCE G
Lowering position
FORCE J
FORCE S Areas cleared of mines
EASTERN TASK FORCE
(BRITISH)
Ramillies Warspite
Z
Northern Limit
of Assault Area
Le Grand
Clos

Ship type	R.N. R.C.N.	U.S.N.	Allied Navies
Battleships	4	3	–
Monitors	2	–	–
Cruisers	21	3	3
Destroyers	116	40	8
TOTALS	**143**	**46**	**11**

Allied Ships Involved in the Naval Bombardment 5–6 June 1944

German gun points towards
the Channel. By early 1942
gun emplacements dotted the
coastline of occupied Europe
from the tip of Norway to the
western end of France's
border with Spain

3 WALK-OVER AT UTAH, BLOODSHED AT OMAHA

Forces Assigned to Operation Neptune

Status	Amount
Naval Combat Vessels	1,213
Landing Ships and Craft	4,126
Ancillary Craft	736
Merchant Ships	864
TOTALS	**6,939**

At 3.00 a.m., the first of the American assault force – nine battalions of the 4th Infantry Division – began to pack into the smaller landing craft from their transports. Rear Admiral Alan Kirk, commander of the Western Task Force, had ordered the 1,000 ships to heave-to almost 12 miles out at sea to keep them well clear of German shore batteries. The stiff 18-knot breeze whipped up a four-foot swell, which made the landing craft lurch; the men, in their carapaces of equipment, had a terrible time transferring from the transports. Many mistimed their jumps, injuring themselves badly. Several fell overboard to their deaths. Under way, the men were soon covered in spray and ashen with seasickness. They were in for three and a half miserable hours.

Dawn that morning was at 5.58 a.m., grim, gray and windy. A leading

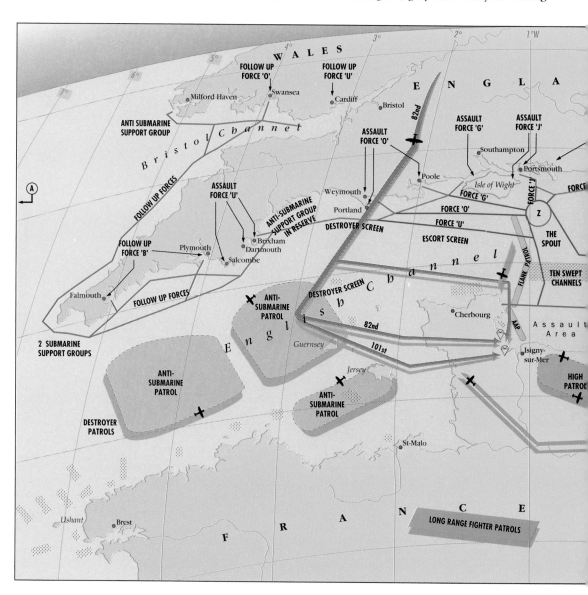

patrol craft and one of the LC'Ts hit mines. But from behind, above and ahead came the boom and crash of warships pounding the German fortifications, the explosions as the shells struck, and the deep drone of 360 heavy bombers and 269 medium bombers. In fact, it became clear later that it was only the naval bombardment that did any real damage. The heavy bombers were above the clouds and 67 of them never released their bombs; the rest, bombing blind, overshot the coastal targets to avoid hitting the incoming forces. The medium bombers made few direct hits.

As the landing craft approached, the rain of fire lifted from the beach to the dunes and grasslands beyond. The troops were due to land at 6.30 a.m - H-Hour, in military terminology - just after low tide, so that the demolition teams could deal with the beach obstacles before the tide covered them. Their beach, codenamed Utah, was the most westerly of the five assault beaches, and therefore was the first to receive the incoming tide as it advanced up the Channel. They would start the invasion with their

Personnel Assigned to Operation Neptune

	U.S.	U.K.	Other Allies
Warships	20,380	78,244	4,988
L/ships crafts & barges	30,009	32,880	–
Naval shore & misc. parties	2,500	1,700	
Sub/Tot	52,889	112,824	4,988
Total Allied Navies		170,701	
Allied Merchant Navies		25,000	
TOTAL		**195,701**	

Aircraft Assigned to Operation Neptune

VARIOUS COMMANDS

2nd Tactical Airforce USAAF 8th Airforce USAAF 9th Airforce	
Fighters	5050
Heavy Bombers	3460
Light/Med bombers	1650
Transport aircraft	2310
Gliders	2600
Recce/scouts	700
U.S. TOTAL	6080
Allied/British	5510
GRAND TOTAL	**11,590**

On the 6 June Allied airforces flew 14,674 missions and lost 127 aircraft. The German reply was a mere 319 missions against the Allied forces

An Allied convoy makes its way down the "spout" to the assault area. Barrage balloons gave some protection from expected low-level German air attacks. Such was the strength of Allied air cover they were little needed

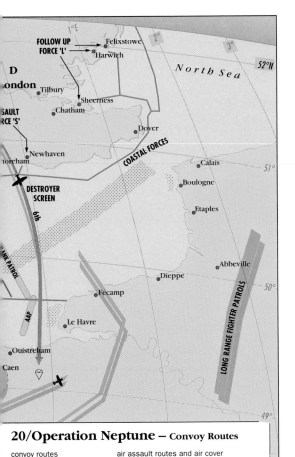

20/Operation Neptune – Convoy Routes

convoy routes

—— swept channels:

—— Neptune channels

British minefields

German minefields

air assault routes and air cover

patrols (AAP-assault area patrols)

high air patrol

night fighter patrol lines

air assault routes

drop zones

colleagues on Omaha, 10 miles to the east. Both would be in action before the British, who would be riding in with the tide an hour later on the eastern beaches.

Behind Utah stood seven German strongpoints, with another 20 batteries strung out further along the coast. In one of the strongpoints, W5, which guarded the road leading inland to Ste-Marie-du-Mont, was Lieutenant Arthur Jahnke, shaken by the bombs and shells but at least alive. As the bombardment moved away inland, he found several of his men dead, the telephones down, his guns destroyed. All he and his survivors had were two machine guns, a mortar and a few rifles. He stared out of the slit and over the beach. There, beyond the low concrete wall, the lines of stakes, the obstacles and the mines, he saw the first landing craft approaching. Numbly, he and his surviving men picked up their paltry weapons.

Some 300 yards from the shore, the leading commanders fired smoke flares to stop the bombardment. The men saw the flying sand, earth, smoke and dust fall away and drift clear along the low-lying and featureless shore. At 6.31 a.m. just a minute behind schedule, the first 10 landing craft lowered their ramps and 300 men of the 8th Infantry Regiment's 2nd Battalion stepped into waist-deep water and waded the 100 yards to the water's edge. Within minutes they were joined by the 1st Battalion. Ahead lay a quarter-mile stretch of sand scattered with angular obastacles. It was oddly quiet. No one had fired a shot.

One reason for the silence was that the few surviving defenders were still dazed by the bombing and lacked links with their commanders; another, that German commanders did not expect an Allied landing here where the flooding seemed to preclude mobility. But mainly the silence was because the Americans were in the wrong place. With the leading patrol craft sunk by a mine, there had been no clear guidance on the final run-in. A powerful current had dragged the force to the left, to a spot about a mile south of the intended landing site, and one that was by chance almost unprotected, except by Jahnke's W5 blockhouse.

A final factor was the Germans' pure astonishment at the sight that then unfolded. Twelve ungainly objects that looked to Jahnke like giant bath-tubs crawled out of the water. Sixteen others were floundering through the breakers. As he watched, the first arrivals proceeded to drop their canvas sides, revealing themselves to be 33-ton Sherman tanks. They were to have been launched four miles offshore, but to avoid the heavy swell they took to the water only two miles out, and came in as intended with the infantry. There was nothing in Jahnke's training to prepare him for this. Tanks were not meant to come out of the sea. Amphibious assaults were meant to provide only soft targets. These were anything but. Several of them opened fire on W5, knocking out one of the machine-gun posts and a mortar.

Jahnke, in desperation, tried a little-used weapon – wire-controlled miniature tanks carrying 200 pounds of explosive. In theory, the Goliaths, as they were derisorily named by the Germans themselves, could crawl for some 600 yards and be detonated by remote control. In practice, their electrical systems were disrupted and not one of them worked properly. They wandered about randomly to the amusement of the Americans, until they ran out of fuel. Only one went off when a group of soldiers placed a grenade by it. The explosion tore the men to pieces. The rest of the Goliaths were defused by demolition experts later.

Jahnke's blockhouse now drew the attention of the only general to land with the Americans, Brigadier General Theodore Roosevelt. The eldest son of the former president and cousin of the present one, he was already something of a legend. At 57 he was supposedly too old for action, but he

American soldiers ready themselves aboard a landing craft off Normandy

had persuaded the 4th's commander, General Raymond Barton, that he could "steady the boys." He did, too (though this was to be his last campaign: he died of a heart attack on 12 July). As the landing force built up on the beach, he led 600 men against Jahnke's W5 strongpoint. A direct hit on the pillbox followed by a determined attack put W5 and Jahnke himself out of the war. Though badly wounded, Jahnke survived as a captive in England. He returned to the beach in 1987, by which time W5 had been rebuilt with a different role as part of the Utah Beach Museum.

Roosevelt, strolling about waving a cane, now had a tactical problem – 30,000 men and 3,500 vehicles were due to land on Utah shortly and he was in the wrong place. Here there was only one road inland. There was likely to be a monumental traffic jam. On the other hand the road was now clear, while the four roads further north were still guarded. He decided to stay where he was, and "start the war from here."

It proved to be a good decision. By the time the German defences had zeroed-in on this section of the beach, the invasion was well under way. After an hour, demolition experts had begun to clear the mined obstacles from the shallows for the incoming landing craft. The Americans had rejected the use of the "funnies," and didn't miss them. After two and half hours the tanks were through the Atlantic Wall and fanning out in a two-mile front. Behind them, the landing began to seem routine. To some, it all seemed something of an anti-climax. One by one the strongpoints that had been the original targets fell. A log-jam of vehicles queued to cross the causeways, slowed by occasional shells.

By the end of the day, as the men surged inland to link up with the paratroopers, the assault force had landed 23,250 men and 1,700 vehicles for the loss of 197 with 60 missing presumed drowned. Losses ten times that figure would have been acceptable.

Meanwhile, ten miles away on Omaha, a four-mile sweep of sand and

American landing craft approach the beachhead with their loads of nervous, eager and seasick soldiers

21/Utah Landings

- ▲ landing craft
- H+5 wave landing times
- ● German coastal defences
- ◀ German strongpoint
- ▨ concentrated German forces
- ‧‧‧‧‧ 'hedgehogs'
- — tank ditch
- ⁓ mines
- ‧⁓‧ barbed wire
- ⁓⁓ dunes

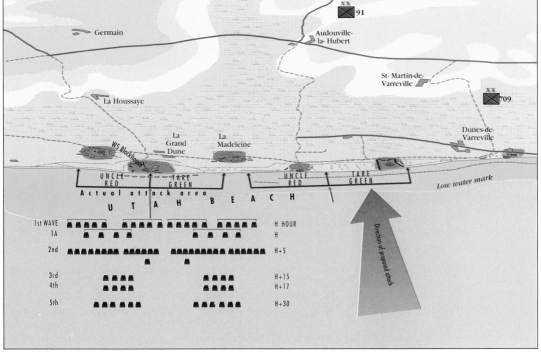

XX
91

Germain

Audouville-
la- Hubert

St- Martin-de-
Varreville

La Houssaye

XX
709

La
Grand
Dune

La
Madeleine

Dunes-de-
Varreville

W5 Blockhouse

UNCLE
RED
TARE
GREEN

UNCLE
RED
TARE
GREEN

Low water mark

Actual attack area

U T A H   B E A C H

1st WAVE			H HOUR	
1A			H	
2nd			H+5	
3rd			H+15	
4th			H+17	
5th			H+30	

Direction of proposed attack

shingle, terrible things were happening. There, losses were to be almost 20 times those on Utah.

Omaha, the only gap in 20 miles of cliffs that separated Utah from the British beaches, was not a promising landing site for an amphibious assault. Flanked by 100-foot cliffs, it was backed by a steep pebble bank and dunes. Beyond the bank and dunes was an open 200-yard expanse of salt-marsh which ended in a 150-foot escarpment divided at four points by ravines, or "draws" as the Americans called them. Vehicles would have a hard time reaching the four tracks that led inland through the ravines, even without opposition.

There would be opposition in plenty, for it was an easy beach to defend, and an obvious assault point. Mined obstacles – iron frames, wooden stakes set at an angle, steel hedgehogs that would hole incoming craft – littered the shallows. The dunes were topped with barbed wire and a concrete wall. Anti-tank ditches criss-crossed the salt marsh, which was well mined. From the cliffs at either end, 75mm and 88mm guns could rake the beach from behind walls three feet thick. Facing the beach, mostly huddling round the four tracks, was a line of strongpoints – eight big-gun emplacements, 35 pill-boxes, 18 anti-tank guns, 85 machine-gun nests.

Behind all this lay another line of defence – a coast road along which lay three villages to which the tracks led. At the western end, guarding a paved track, lay Vierville. In the center, dominating two tracks, was St-Laurent, while the eastern track led to Colleville. All these would have to be taken if the invaders were ever to get their men and vehicles off the beach. Even then, there was a final obstacle – the flooded valley of the River Aure.

Omaha would at best be a tough nut. But not suicidal, according to Intelligence. True, the invaders would be doing precisely what the Dieppe Raid had warned them not to do – assaulting a well-defended beach head-on. And the Americans would not have the backing of the British "funnies," which Bradley's commanders felt would demand too much special training and were anyway untried. The troops, however, were very well tried. Leading the assault would be three regiments of the Ist Division, known as the Big Red One, veterans of North Africa and Sicily. They would be fighting alongside the 29th Division's 116th Regiment. This battle-hardened force would sup-posedly be confronted by no more than 1,000 men of the 716th Infantry Division, mostly Polish or Russian conscripts who were not expected to show fight-to-the-death commitment. Dash, courage, experience, over-whelming numbers and two battalions of DD tanks – some 60 in all – would carry the day.

Utah Beach, American troops supporting those already landed, plunge into the surf and wade shoreward, heavily laden with equipment including medical supplies

Perhaps they might have done. What the Allies did not know, however, was that part of the 352nd Infantry Division, tough veterans of the Eastern Front, had moved up from St-Lô several weeks before, doubling the number of defenders from four battalions to eight, and vastly increasing the defenders' capabilities. By an odd coincidence, they had just completed an anti-invasion exercise and were thus more than ready to counter the American landing. General Bradley was told of the move just as the convoy was sailing – too late to do anything about it. This combination of natural obstacles, strong fortifications and tough defenders would have given the most optimistic commander second thoughts.

On top of this came the weather, and the consequences of poor planning. At Omaha, the decision to load up the landing craft so far from the shore would prove disastrous. The transports were more exposed than those off Utah, and the seas were rougher. The stormy twelve-mile journey would be even worse than the run-in to Utah. So it proved. Loading in the dark between 3.00 and 4.00 a.m., ten of the transports, each carrying some 300 men, were swamped. Many of the men sank screaming, weighed down by their packs. All 26 artillery guns went to the bottom in their DUKWs. For the rest, it was the start of a grim, wet and sickly voyage. One colonel recalled later how some of the men "just lay there with the water sloshing back and forth over them, not caring whether they lived or died."

Then, almost four miles offshore, the time came to launch the DD tanks. The result was nightmarish. Of the 29 intended for the eastern end of the beach, 24 drove down their ramps into the wind-whipped water. Rapidly, the waves overwhelmed the canvas sides and battered down the supports of 21 of them, which sank like steel coffins, taking almost all their crews with them. One was sunk by a landing craft, two fell victims to German guns. Another three were beached later, from a landing craft with a damaged ramp.

22/Utah Beach

♂♂	light machine guns
⌐	barbed wire
ᴛᴀᴛᴀᴛᴀᴛ	'hedgehogs'
ᴡᴡᴡᴡ	tank ditch
⊖	mines
-----	track

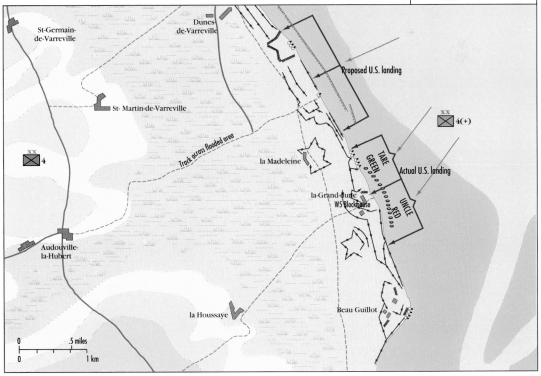

The U.S. advance from the beaches was often very slow and nearly always precarious. This G.I. tests a suspected German position by raising his helmet above the hedge

When the appalled officers in charge of the 32 DDs destined for the western sector saw what was happening, they kept the tanks aboard to be beached later. Only two of the 24 that were launched to cover the Infantry made it to shore with the troops.

As with the force then approaching Utah, the invaders took heart from the accompanying bombardment – the salvos of rockets launched from the approaching fleet, the booms and flashes as the battleships *Texas* and *Arkansas* opened up behind them, the drone of the Eighth Air Force Fortresses above, and the crash of exploding bombs ahead. "There would be a flash like a blast furnace from the 14-inch guns," wrote the novelist Ernest Hemingway, who was riding into action on board a landing craft,

"And with the smoke still rolling, the concussion and the report ... struck your ear like a punch with a heavy, dry glove.

Then up on the green rise of a hill that now showed clearly as we moved in would spout two tall black fountains of earth and smoke.

'Look what they're doing to those Germans,' I leaned forward to hear a G.I. say above the roar of the motor. 'I guess there won't be a man alive there'."

How wrong he was. As at Utah, the heavy bombers delayed their drops by a few vital seconds. Their 13,000 bombs fell on the fields, doing absolutely no damage to the Germans guarding the beaches. And with the low cloud, the dust and the smoke, the naval gunners had difficulty finding targets. The bombardment killed a great many fish, and precious few of the enemy.

The Germans watched. Five miles inland, the battery officer of the 105mm howitzers at Houteville stood ready, telephone to ear, waiting for the order to open fire.

The first wave – 1,450 men in 36 landing craft – approached on schedule, at 06.30 a.m., the coxswains fighting to maneuvre their ungainly craft through the labyrinth of angular steel obstacles and wooden stakes. They were almost dead in the water, targets as perfect as beached whales.

From a quarter of a mile away, from the strongpoint directly in front of the lead landing craft, came the first burst of machine-gun fire. Others followed. The Americans heard the unnerving sound of bullets clanging on the steel hulls. At the same moment, howitzer shells from Houteville landed, screaming in to blast the beach with sand and flying shrapnel.

The 116th, taking the right (western) sector, were the first out, at 6.36 a.m. As the ramps of the first four landing craft went down, the men saw the shallows ahead whipped white by bullets. The beach is still known as Bloody Omaha, and it was bloody from the first seconds when the first men who lumbered down the ramps into waist-deep water became the first to die in the inferno of cross fire from artillery, mortars, machine guns and rifles.

The history of the 116th prepared by the US War Department captures the horror of it: "As the first men [of Company A] jumped, they crumpled and flopped into the water. Then order was lost. It seemed to the men that the only way to get ashore was to dive in head first and swim clear of the fire that was striking the boats. But as they hit the water, their heavy equipment dragged them down, and soon they were fighting to keep afloat." Those who survived drowning and the bullets to drag themselves ashore found no shelter, except the sea, and many crawled back into the scant protection of the breaking waves. Within 10 minutes every officer and sergeant had been either killed or wounded. The living edged in with the rising tide, sometimes sheltering behind metal obstacles or wooden stakes, hauling on their floundering companions to save them from drowning, only to see them hit, only to be hit themselves. Within 20 minutes, Company A was nothing more than a "forlorn little rescue party bent upon survival."

Behind Company A and the assault company of 16th Infantry came wave after wave of other troops, all piling into the carnage, and all mixed up. The current, the smoke, the noise, the maze of obstacles, the crush of boats and corpses scrambled plans and command structures. The 270 engineers (half of whom had been killed or wounded) struggled to clear lanes through the obstacles, obstacles being used as shelter by their own troops. They were supposed to clear sixteen 50-yard paths in precisely 27 minutes. In fact, in

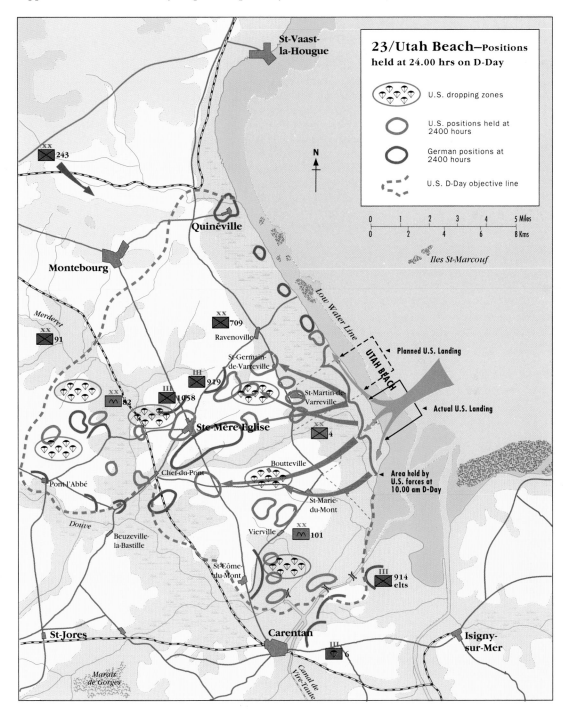

23/Utah Beach–Positions held at 24.00 hrs on D-Day

- U.S. dropping zones
- U.S. positions held at 2400 hours
- German positions at 2400 hours
- U.S. D-Day objective line

that time, they managed to mark only one route (and only six in all before the tide halted their work). As landing craft crowding into the single corridor dropped their ramps, men ran, jumped and dived out to almost certain death. All along the beach, landing craft sank or exploded as they hit mines or as artillery shells detonated ammunition stacked on deck. One sergeant saw an assault boat hit a mined obstacle and explode into fragments, throwing up a headless torso which landed by him with a sickening thud.

Ashore, the dead and wounded, sitting and lying in the dead calm of shock, were scattered across the sand and shallows. One man sat at the water's edge throwing stones into the water, "crying softly as if his heart would break."

For the 29th Division, the experience was particularly tragic. As opposed to the usual random allocation of men to units, the 29th was formed of so-called Pals companies, men who were recruited together from the same areas. In the division's Ist Battalion, the first three companies came from Virginia – from the communities of Bedford, Lynchburg and Roanoke. Bedford, a village of 3,000, lost 23 men that day, 22 of them from 116th's Company A, among them three sets of brothers. Two of them were Raymond and Bedford Hoback. Raymond was wounded, and lay on the beach until the sea washed over him and drowned him. His body was never found, but his Bible was. A G.I. picked it up next day and mailed it to his family, who meanwhile had had two telegrams on consecutive days telling them of their loss.

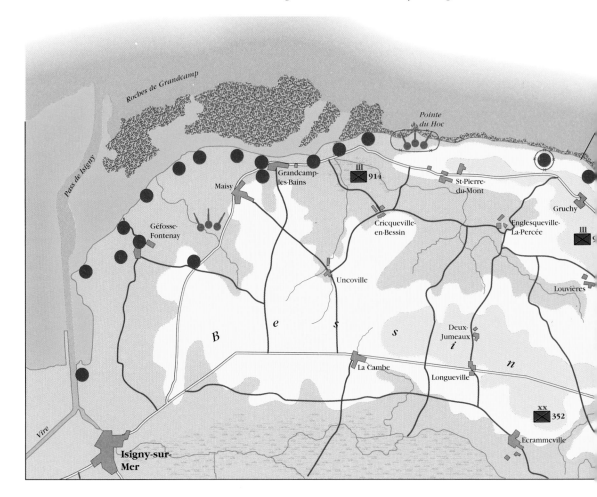

The only shelter on Omaha was a narrow shelf of shale and shingle a few yards wide halfway across the beach. As the troops pressed forward from the shallows, as the tide crept in, as the beach became littered with ammunition, gas-masks, buckled radio sets, tools, all the detritus of war, the shingle shelf clogged into a solid mass of bodies, both living and dead. No one could move. Group leaders could not co-ordinate a response, especially among the unseasoned 29th. All momentum – that most prized of elements in battle – was lost. A terrible paralysis threatened.

Four miles to the west, there had been success, of a sort. Up on the cliffs of a 100-foot headland, Pointe du Hoc, was the most formidable of the coastal batteries. According to Intelligence, it contained six 155mm guns, which could fire 14 miles, far enough to threaten both the fleet and the landing. The *Texas* and the *Arkansas* had pumped 600 shells on to the battery. Now 225 men of the 2nd Ranger Battalion, seconded to 116th Infantry, had the task of scaling the cliffs and destroying the guns (the battery might have been targeted by the paras during the night, but they would not have had the advantage of a pre-assault bombardment).

The Rangers set out in ten British-crewed landing craft, aiming to reach the small rocky beach at the foot of the cliffs before the first landings on Omaha. Three of the landing craft sank, and a fierce current carried the rest too far to the east. By the time they had worked their way back along the coast they were late and the invasion had been under way for 40 minutes.

The plan had been to use DUKWs fitted with fire ladders, but the beach was so cratered by shells that the vehicles could not operate. Instead, men shot rope ladders and rope-bearing grapnels on to the cliff-top. They began to climb into the teeth of withering fire, and grenades rolled down from the top by the 200 defenders, men of the 716th Coastal Defence Division.

At first, many Rangers died, sliding and bouncing to their deaths. Some,

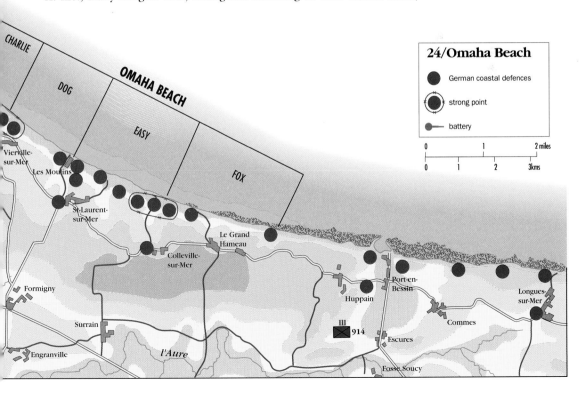

Storming ashore at Omaha
Beach – the first wave of
Americans landing on what
was to be the most difficult of
the invasion beaches to take.
For many hours they were
close to defeat

though, used their own grenades to blast shelter and hand holds in the cliff-face. And help was at hand – in the form of some accurate shelling from two destroyers, the American *Satterlee* and the British *Talybont* (the craters are still there today, around the battery that has been converted into a Ranger Memorial). Above, most of the defenders scattered, and the surviving Rangers hauled themselves over the cliff-edge to seize the battery and take captive the remaining enemy troops.

To their chagrin, the Rangers then discovered the guns were not even in the battery. Under security so strict that not even the French Resistance knew of the operation, they had been hidden in an orchard a kilometer inland. There, the Rangers found them and destroyed them.

They were to hold the point for the next two days, despite fierce counterattacks, and despite a misdirected bombing raid from Allied planes. In this brave, bitterly fought contest, the Rangers lost 135 of their 225 men in what some have called a fruitless operation. In the end, though, they served a purpose quite different from that intended, attracting the attention of the counterattacking 914th Regiment, which would otherwise have turned on the beaches, perhaps with devastating consequences.

On the beach itself, the remaining tanks had begun to haul themselves ashore from their LCTs. Hemingway watched from his landing craft:

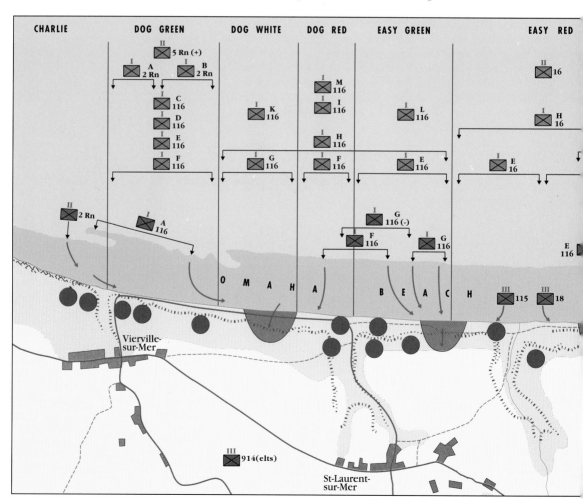

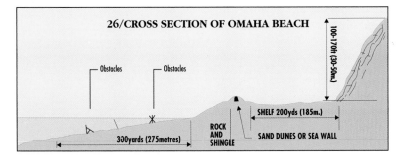

26/CROSS SECTION OF OMAHA BEACH

100-170ft (30-50m.)

Obstacles   Obstacles

SHELF 200yds (185m.)

300yards (275metres)

ROCK AND SHINGLE

SAND DUNES OR SEA WALL

"One of the tanks flared up and started to burn with thick black smoke and yellow flames. Farther down the beach, another tank started burning. Along the line of the beach, they were crouched like big yellow toads along the high water mark. As I stood up watching, two more started to burn. The first ones were pouring out gray smoke now, and the wind was blowing it flat along the beach. As I stood up, trying to see if there was anyone beyond the high water line of tanks, one of the burning tanks blew up with a flash in the steaming gray smoke.

The first, second, third, fourth and fifth waves lay where they had

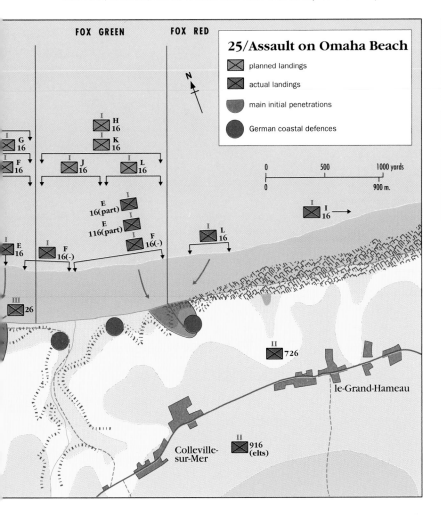

FOX GREEN   FOX RED

25/Assault on Omaha Beach

◨ planned landings

◨ actual landings

▬ main initial penetrations

⬤ German coastal defences

0   500   1000 yards
0   900 m.

le-Grand-Hameau

Colleville-sur-Mer

Taking cover beneath a sea obstacle on Omaha. German bullets whipped the beach and shallows with such ferocity that soldiers took cover wherever they could fallen, looking like so many heavily laden bundles on the flat, pebbly stretch between the sea and the first cover ... I saw three tanks coming along the beach, barely moving, they were advancing so slowly. The Germans let them cross the open space where the valley opened onto the beach, and it was absolutely flat, with a perfect field of fire. Then I saw a little fountain of water jut up, just over and beyond the lead tank. Then smoke broke out of the leading tank on the side away from us, and I saw two men dive out of the turret and land on their hands and knees on the stones of the beach. They were close enough so that I could see their faces, but no more men came out as the tank started to blaze up and burn furiously."

That was what it looked like to Hemingway, who had an injured knee and never made it ashore. One of the war correspondents who captured it was photographer Robert Capa, of *Life* magazine. "If your pictures aren't good, you're not close enough," he used to say, so there was no question of standing back. When he went ashore with the 16th Regiment his first thoughts were not of death, but of how ugly war had made such a beautiful spot. Taking shots all the time, he came in across 100 yards of sand with men falling all around him, finally taking refuge briefly behind a burnt-out tank. Out in the open again, mortars screamed in and he hugged the sand surrounded by terrified G.I.'s. As he lay there, pinned down by noise and flying sand, he felt "a new kind of fear shaking my body from toe to hair, and twisting my face." Trying to reload his Contax camera, he found he couldn't. His hands were trembling too much. Reacting in pure, unthinking emotion, he stood and ran to a landing craft. He realized he was running away, hesitated, but couldn't face the beach again. As he climbed on board, there was an explosion. "The skipper was crying. His assistant had been blown up all over him, and he was a mess." The landing craft delivered him, along with a mass of other wounded men, to the USS *Chase* from where he rejoined the advance inland later.

He had taken almost three rolls of film, 106 pictures. They were rushed to *Time*'s London office. There, a darkroom assistant, eager to see the best visual record of Omaha, perhaps of the whole invasion, dried the negatives too quickly. He melted the emulsion, and ruined almost all the three films. Only ten shots survived.

Few were in any position to analyze what was happening, but if they had it would have seemed that Rommel was about to achieve his aim of crushing the invasion before it got off the beaches. For a while, that was also the judgment of General Bradley, twelve and a half miles offshore in the USS *Augusta*. By 9.00 a.m., he had "gained the impression our troops had suffered an irreversible catastrophe." He sent a message to SHAEF asking permission to transfer the rest of his force to the British beaches, leaving those ashore to their fate. The message did not reach SHAEF until late afternoon. By then, it had become irrelevent.

For the incoming tide of the assault had begun at last to make ground. Lone individuals, driven by desperation to acts of great bravery, got things moving, creating breaches in the German defences in three places on the far left and right wings.

By 10.00 a.m., along with a few hardy Rangers, some 200 men of the 116th's 1st Battalion took advantage of smoke from burning grass set on fire by the naval bombardment to ease through barbed wire and minefields, scale the bluff leading to the gently rolling plateau of farmland, and run into Vierville, half a mile inland.

A mile to the east, men of the 2nd and 3rd Battalions, using gas masks against the pall of smoke, discovered a minefield that had been largely destroyed by the bombardment, and edged over the bluff towards St-Laurent.

At the far eastern end of Omaha, part of the 16th Infantry had side-slipped off course when landing and found themselves clear of the strongpoints protecting the approach to Colleville. They climbed a steep ravine in the cliffs, fought through light defences, and around 9.30 a.m. set off along the cliff-top towards Port-en-Bessin, intending to link up with the most westerly of the British beaches, 10 miles away.

In the center, though, the remains of the 16th's 1st and 2nd Battalions lay amid bullets and shells in the lee of the shingle shelf, with its crest of concrete and barbed wire. At last, a lieutenant and a sergeant, taking their lives in their hands, walked out to inspect the wire. The lieutenant returned (as the U.S. official history relates) and "hands on hips, looked down disgustedly" at the men lying behind the shingle bank. "Are you going to lie there and get killed, or get up and do something about it?" Nobody stirred, so the sergeant and the lieutenant got the materials and blew the wire. That gave the men heart enough to file through the gap and on through a minefield. Many were hit, many others fell victims to mines, but by about 10.00 a.m., some 300 were up the bluff and fighting their way to Colleville, damning to hell Normandy's network of hedges, ditches and small fields, the beginnings of the bocage that gave snipers such perfect cover.

That still left most of the men trapped on the beach, which was rapidly clogging with vehicles. Something had to be done fast, not only to lift the immediate threat, but to ensure that the Americans had a secure foothold before the Germans could send reinforcements.

In fact, reinforcements were slow in coming. 84th Corps had scant information about what was happening. General Marcks thought the British posed a greater threat and that was where he told the tanks to go. Marcks' reserves, the 915th Regiment, had set off before dawn in pursuit of what turned out to be a stick of dummy parachutists, and would not be back for hours. Meanwhile, the troops that might have turned the battle on the beach in the Germans' favor were squandered in the pointless counterattacks on the Rangers on the Pointe du Hoc.

From the beach, the 1st Division's commander, Colonel George Taylor, sent a message to Major General Clarence Huebner on board his headquarters ship out at sea: "There are too many vehicles on the beach; send

American troops land under heavy fire from German positions on the bluffs above Omaha Beach

combat troops. 30 LCT's waiting offshore; cannot come in because of shelling." Huebner responded at once, suspending the flow of everything but troops – the 18th Infantry – and tanks, and calling for increased naval bombardment of German strongpoints.

On the *Texas*, Rear Admiral Bryant shouted over the radio: "Get on them, men! Get on them! They're raising hell with the men on the beach, and we can't have any more of that! We must stop it!" Destroyers moved inland to within 800 yards of the shore – into waters so shallow they occasionally touched bottom – swung broadside, and delivered salvo after salvo.

At 11.00 a.m. the tide of battle began to turn. Taylor, in one of the day's most famous incidents, yelled down the beach: "Two kinds of people are going to stay on this beach, the dead and those who are going to die. Now, let's get the hell out of here!" Then, as three DD tanks blasted the German emplacement ahead, he led an advance through wire and minefields, with wounded men not daring to move themselves yelling warnings about un-exploded mines.

An hour and a half after landing in Taylor's wake, the 18th advanced uphill, over the plateau and on into Colleville where the 16th were already fighting house-to-house. Steadily, other strongpoints fell. By late afternoon, as the engineers at last cleared ways through the minefields, the first vehicles crawled off the beach along the Colleville track in support of the infantry.

As dusk approached, several units of the 1st Division's 115th and 116th Infantry Regiments cut their way to and then across the second line of

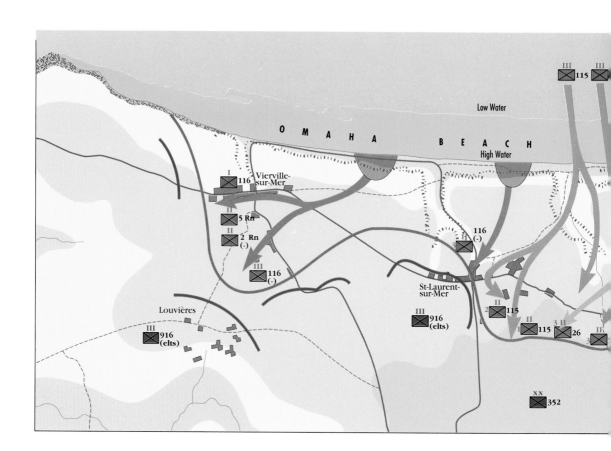

defence, the coast road linking the three villages behind Omaha. St-Laurent was under sustained attack. A mile and a half to the west, Vierville was in American hands. By nightfall, the beachhead, protecting over 30,000 men already crowded into the beach area, was a patchwork of American-held pockets scattered over an area six miles long and two miles deep. It was a far cry from the ambitions of the morning, but it was at least a toe-hold.

Bloody Omaha has become a classic of near-disaster, analyzed almost to the point of sterility. As often, hindsight has allowed armchair strategists to judge leadership harshly. The long run into the beach; the refusal to accept specialized vehicles; the unnecessary loss of the tanks; the direct assault on strongpoints; the congestion – all of this suggests a sort of purblind arrogance, very different from the flexibility and realism displayed by British and American commanders later in the campaign. It was as if Dieppe counted for nothing. Indeed, it could have been different; but probably not very different. Omaha had to be assaulted, and there was nothing to be done about the weather or the defences. Omaha would have been bloody however it was attacked.

At the end of D-Day, 3,000 Americans lay dead, and the hold on Omaha was precarious. The units were so scattered that there was no proper front line, and thus no chance of support from the battleships and cruisers out to sea. If German tanks arrived, the Americans could still be overwhelmed. Their fate depended now on success elsewhere, especially on the British beaches to the east.

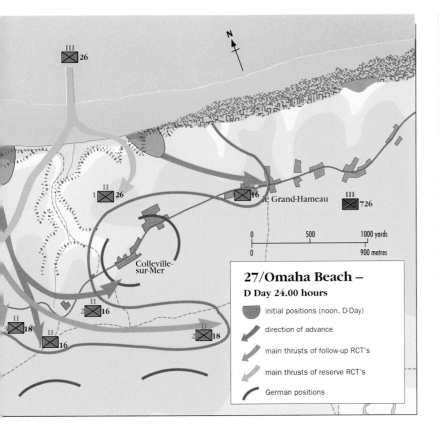

27/Omaha Beach –
D Day 24.00 hours

- initial positions (noon, D-Day)
- direction of advance
- main thrusts of follow-up RCT's
- main thrusts of reserve RCT's
- German positions

D-Day plus one – American "follow-up" troops wade ashore to reinforce units moving inland from the bridgehead

4 GOLD, JUNO AND SWORD: THE STRUGGLE FOR FOOTHOLDS

Madam d'Anselm lived on the sea front in the village of Asnelle, just to the west of the beach designated "Gold" by the Allies. She might have fled, as others did, but she had a husband and a son in the Resistance and she was determined to stay put. She and her family of eight had dug a trench in the garden, with no roof, but big enough to take them all. On the night of 5 June, as they sheltered in their trench, bomb blasts blew out the windows and cracked the walls. In the early hours, the explosions died away and two of the children ran back to the house to fetch something. One of them stood on

Infantry crowd onto the beach after landing. They huddle for a moment crouching low, watching shells burst from the naval bombardment before moving inland

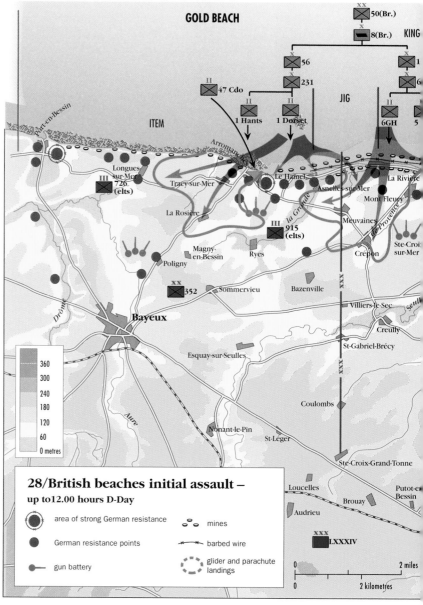

28/British beaches initial assault –
up to 12.00 hours D-Day

- area of strong German resistance
- German resistance points
- gun battery
- mines
- barbed wire
- glider and parachute landings

360
300
240
180
120
60
0 metres

0 — 2 miles
0 — 2 kilometres

the garden wall as moonlight glowed through a gap in the clouds and looked out over the coast. "Maman! Maman!" he shouted, "Look – the sea – its black with boats!"

He was looking at the Eastern Task Force, the ships conveying and protecting General Miles Dempsey's 2nd Army, also known as the British Liberation Army (so called, despite the presence of Canadians). That was perhaps the only few minutes that Mme d'Anselm's son could have stood safely anywhere in Asnelle that day, for those ships were about to deliver a sustained bombardment that would drive French and Germans alike into whatever cover they could find.

In the British and Canadian sectors – 25 miles of beach and perhaps the same of hinterland – the demands, aims, and tactics were all different from those in the American sectors. Here there would sooner or later be a threat that the Americans did not have to face: tanks, in the form of the 21st Panzer

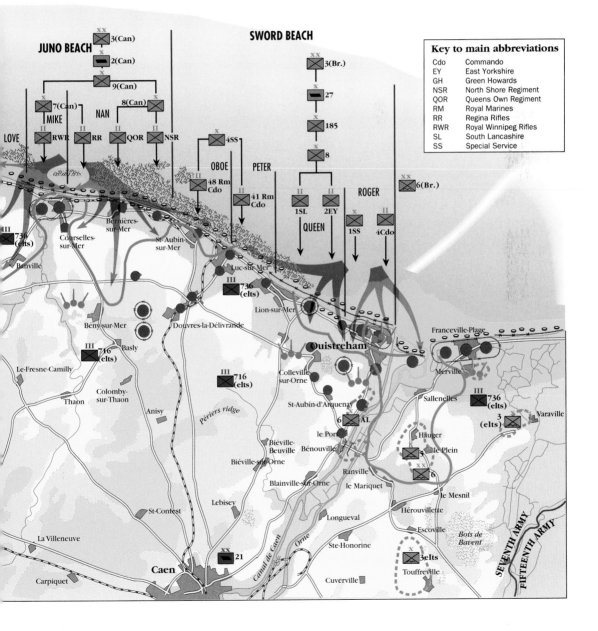

Division, based in Caen. The countryside was more open than the hinterlands of Utah and Omaha, without floods and better for tanks. Not only would the British and Canadians have to take Bayeux and seal the link with the Americans, they would also have to advance rapidly several miles inland to take Caen and secure the eastern flank of the invasion. For that to happen, the vanguard of the 75,000 troops would have to leave the beaches fast, driving hard south and east for up to 20 miles. This was an ambitious aim and increasingly unrealistic in view of the German reinforcements. But Montgomery was determined to preserve this aim to inject drive, momentum and morale into the invasion. To this end, he ordered a longer naval bombardment: two hours. He also made sure the infantry would have the benefit of Hobart's Funnies. Minefields, pillboxes and sea walls could not be allowed to dam the advance.

The bombardment began 40 minutes before sunrise, concentrating on the coastal batteries. Since these had already been bombed during the night, only one answered – the four 6-inch guns buried safe from bombs beneath an immense shield of concrete at Longues. They were not safe, however, from

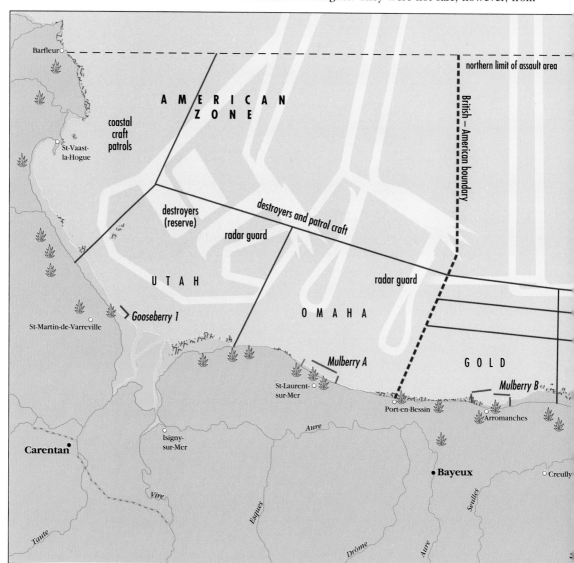

topped with mines. Behind them, the first hails of machine-gun fire and shell-bursts clanged on the leading landing craft. On schedule, at H minus 5 – 7.25 a.m. – the first landing craft nudged through the forest of angle-irons and stakes, many tossed sideways to be ripped or blown apart. The first "crab" tanks rolled ashore and began flailing their way up the beach, the first ramps fell, the first men jumped down into the water.

On all three beaches, the landing was incomparably easier than at Omaha – easier overall, that is, but not everywhere. All along the coast, localized tragedies and horrors turned the landing for some into a universe of chaos, death and for all they knew, imminent failure.

Nevertheless, there was no stopping the momentum. The only threat from the air came when two Lille-based FW-190 fighters – led by a daredevil wing-commander, Josef "Pips" Priller – made a single bold sweep the length of the beaches, guns blazing, banking in and out of barrage balloon cables before zooming back up into the clouds and home. Although the DD tanks were held back because of the heavy seas, the other specialized tanks did double

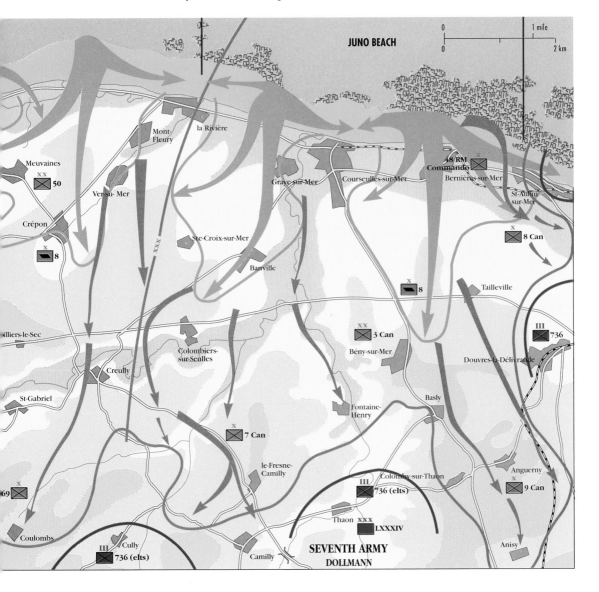

Commandos on the beach near Ouistreham after the landing. In the foreground is the beginning of layers of German barbed wire which proved easier to breach than first thought

duty, clearing minefields and enemy positions alike. In some places, the defenders surrendered quickly, even willingly, for many of the 716th were unwilling Russian and Polish conscripts (and on Sword, four Germans appeared with suitcases packed ready for instant evacuation into capitivity). Within the hour in some places, Churchills had blasted gaps in the sea walls and "crabs" were dissecting minefields with their chains.

To the commanders at sea, to the generals back in England, to politicians in England and Washington, news of the successful landings was like a balm. Eisenhower had been pacing his trailer, occasionally reading a Western. He had done all he could, but there was a chance it would not be enough. He had even scribbled a draft press release in case the worst happened: "Our landings in the Cherbourg–Havre areas have failed … I have withdrawn the troops … If there is any blame or fault attached to the attempt, it is mine alone." Just after 9.30 a.m. he allowed himself to relax. He gave the note to an aide and issued a brief, dry statement that the invasion was under way. With equal relief, the war correspondents could release the "flashes" reporting the landings. Newcasters went on air, newspapers prepared to roll.

All over Britain, and then all over the United States, the tension lifted. In Britain, factories announced the news over loudspeakers, people shouted to neighbors, American soldiers had their hands wrung by strangers. At last, everyone knew where their sons, brothers, fathers and husbands were. In America, dawn had not yet come. At first, only those on nightshift heard the announcement. In a Brooklyn shipyard, hundreds of men and women knelt by the glare of arc lamps on the decks of unfinished Liberty ships and recited the Lord's Prayer. In Philadelphia, the Liberty Bell rang out, and across Virginia - the home of the 29th Division, at that moment emerging from the slaughter on "Bloody" Omaha - the church bells tolled.

On Gold, a shallow arc streaked with soft clay, first ashore were the 1st Battalion of the Hampshires (part of 231st Brigade), preceded by the specialized tanks. The main aim at this, the most westerly beach in the British and Canadian sector, was to seize Bayeux, block the main Bayeux –Caen road to any German tanks heading for the American beaches, and link up with the Americans at Port-en-Bessin. These operations would include securing Arromanches, a fortified village a mile or so west of the beach, because this was to be the anchorage for the other massive Mulberry harbor where the invasion force proper would land in the days to come.

To do all this, they first had to take Le Hamel. A unit of the 352nd overlooking the sea from a sanitorium, which was protected by thick concrete from the naval bombardment, dominated the upper beach. An 88mm Flak 41 - perhaps the most effective and most feared weapon in the German arsenal - had a clear field of fire from a cliff top west of le Hamel. It picked off the leading ship, wrecking its engine room and slewing it round broadside on to the beach. One of the flail tanks, trying to land from this position, sank. Only one managed to beat a path right up the beach. Behind it, landing craft cluttered chaotically at the water's edge.

When the Hampshires stepped clear of the breakers, they found themselves in a confusion of disabled tanks, taking heavy fire from mortars and machine guns, without safe lanes across the beach. They were to lose some 200 men that day. Their battalion commander was wounded, the second-in-command killed. Instead of a direct assault, they turned away east, circling around through Les Roquettes behind Le Hamel. Eventually, a petard - a tank with a huge mortar instead of a gun - lobbed one of its 40-pound "flying dustbins" onto the sanatorium and reduced it to silence.

Further east, away from the reach of the "88", other flail tanks lumbered inland amidst a cloud of exploding mines and flying earth. Behind them, bobbins laid mattresses of coconut over the patches of the soft blue clay, while bridging tanks placed their unwieldy burdens over craters, anti-tank barriers and ditches. Within an hour, the flails had battered four tracks away from the beaches, and petard tanks were reducing fortified houses and strongpoints to rubble. The assault battalion, the 1st Dorsets, drove on towards Arromanches.

Meanwhile, it was the task of the 47th Royal Marine Commandos to capture Port-en-Bessin itself. Initially, they were greeted with heavy machine-gun fire, and lost four out of their 14 assault craft. They actually came ashore east of Le Hamel where there was virtually no enemy fire, worked around the village, and struck westwards for seven miles humping 88 pounds of equipment each. By midday they were out in front of all other units, occupying the high ground above Port-en-Bessin. In the hamlet of St-Côme, halfway up the hill on the way to Arromanches, the church bells cut through the din of gunfire to signal another liberation.

Further along Gold, the East Yorkshire's 5th Battalion and Green Howards' 6th, leading the assault for the 69th Brigade, were off the beach in half an hour, only to be held up briefly at La Rivière – by chance, a corner of the defences had remained undamaged by bombs and shells. An "88" in a massive pillbox only fell silent when a Crab fired directly into its embrasure from 100 yards away.

By 11.00 a.m. there were seven lanes leading away from Gold, and DD tanks, having beached dryshod from their landing craft, were moving inland. Soon after midday the rest of the division was assembling on a beachhead three miles wide by almost as deep.

By that evening, the British at Gold were not far short of their day's objectives. The beachhead was a bulge six miles across, and six miles deep. Bayeux had not been taken as planned, but it was lost to the Germans. All day, despite instructions from the Germans to stay inside, people had gathered excitedly in the cathedral square to listen to a commentary by a priest bellowing down from a vantage point in the tower. Now, advance patrols from the British front just two miles away eased through its almost deserted streets.

German prisoners captured near Sword Beach

To the east, Juno, the five miles between la Rivière and St-Aubin, was in the hands of the Canadians (or rather mostly the Canadians: they were accompanied by the 48th Royal Marine Commandos whose job it was to link up with their colleagues landing further east). According to the Overlord plan, the 3rd Canadian Division, backed by DD tanks, would rush some 11 miles inland, join in the attack on Caen and seize Carpiquet, an airfield five miles west of Caen.

These ambitious aims were undermined from the start by problems that turned Juno into the toughest of the three eastern beaches. The Canadians were scheduled to land at 7.35 a.m. so that the rising tide would carry them over offshore reefs, placing them right in the midst of the mined angle-irons and stakes. Timing was crucial if the demolition teams were to clear paths through the obstacles. But they were delayed another half an hour by the vicious weather, leaving no time for the demolition teams to do their work. In addition, the infantry arrived ahead of the tanks, and the Germans had had extra time to recover from the naval bombardment. Mines and German shells accounted for 90 of the 306 landing craft, as they maneuvered either in or out, and the infantry found themselves horribly exposed.

At Courseulles, a charge by two battalions of the 7th Canadian Brigade –

Royal Winnipegs and the Regina Rifles – overran German defences. But behind them the tide jammed the follow-up forces into a diminishing oblong, despite the best efforts of a formidable bearded beachmaster, Captain Colin Maud, who imposed order with the help of an Alsatian on a chain.

At Bernières, the 8th Canadian Brigade, landing a few minutes after the 7th, also arrived ahead of its tanks, with disastrous results. The assault regiment, the Queen's Own Rifles, had only 100 yards to cover from sea to sea wall, but in that short space half of one company was killed. It took point-blank fire from a gunship and a sharp 15-minute assault to break the defences and open the way inland.

"09.00 hours," ran the diary of the Queen's Own. "Café 100 yards off the beach is open and selling wine." At 11.00, according to the Regina Rifles diary, "old men and women, young girls and children stood in the littered street, clapped their hands, waved the troops on their way and tossed roses in their path." Less than an hour later, the reserves, 9th Brigade, landed in a shambles of troops, bicycles, vehicles and tanks, but without taking a single shot. German gunners on the road south – part of 21st Panzer's anti-tank brigade – held up the advance for several hours, but it was the sheer weight of traffic on the beach that slowed the main Canadian force.

By the end of the day, the Canadians had linked with the British on Gold, making a joint bridgehead 12 miles wide, and were three or four miles short of Caen and Carpiquet – further forward than any other division that day, and almost where they wanted to be.

Almost, but not quite. More seriously, they had not linked with the British on their left at Sword. The 48th Commandos, whose job it was to close the gap, stalled in Langrune, a heavily fortified town a mile east of Juno, where mines, barbed wire and concrete sealed off every street and provided superb cover for the defenders. It would take artillery and tanks another day to blast a way through. Between Juno and Sword, then there remained a corridor two to four miles wide which offered an opening for the greatest single German threat – the tanks of 21st Panzers, then belatedly rolling up to halt the British advance and split the Allied front from Caen to the sea.

All morning bombs, shells and the Resistance action deprived the German command of its eyes, ears and voice. Those with direct responsibility – from local commanders up to operations staff at Rommel's Army Group B in Roche-Guyon and Rundstedt's OB West in Paris – knew now this was a major assault. Those not on the spot, far away in Germany, still expected a greater and more dangerous landing in the Calais area. The whole upper command structure was shackled by Hitler's system of personal authority. Nobody could move without him, and he was deeply committed to the preservation of interlinking fantasies: that the landings were a feint, that the Third Reich was impregnable, and that only he knew how to defend it.

In the small hours, General Marcks had alerted 7th Army in Le Mans. The 7th Army had passed on the news to Army Group B and OB West. There were two vital decisions to be made. The 21st Panzers, only four miles from the British troops, had to be thrown into action; and the two reserve tank divisions, 12th SS Hitler Youth in Evreux and Panzer Lehr south of Chartres, should be set in motion westwards. The tanks had 80 miles or more to go. The sooner they started the better.

There could be no rapid response. Of the five senior commanders, three were away from their HQ's and another, Geyr von Schweppenburg, had been deprived of operational command. The remaining commander, Rundstedt, did indeed ask for Hitler's permission to release the Panzer reserves.

In his mountain retreat at Berchtesgaden, Hitler slept. When his Chief

An American-made Sherman tank equipped with the British 17-pounder gun. This conversion known as the "Firefly" is seen landing from an L.S.T.

of Operations, General Alfred Jodl, was told of Rundstedt's request by his deputy, he prevaricated. "It could be a diversionary attack," he said, and refused to disturb Hitler.

Rommel himself, preparing to set out from his home to see Hitler, did not learn how serious the situation was until 10.15 a.m. (11.15 British time), when his chief of staff, Major-General Hans Speidel, phoned him with news of the landings. Suddenly Rommel saw the truth of what was happening. "How stupid of me," he said quietly, replaced the receiver, cancelled his meeting with Hitler and prepared for the long drive to France.

General Edgar Feuchtinger, commanding the 21st Panzers in Caen, was in the most invidious position. His tanks were closest to the invaders. He if anyone might have thrown them back into the sea. He had known of the paratroop landings in the Caen area since the early hours. He had 16,000 men, 146 tanks, some 50 mobile assault guns, four motorized infantry battalions, an anti-aircraft battalion and an anti-tank battalion with 24 88mm guns dug in to the north of Caen. All were geared for action. But officially he could do nothing until ordered to by Rommel, commander of Army Group B. Orders might also have come from lower down the chain of command, but that chain was a tangle of broken links. Was he to expect orders from the still incomplete HQ of 47th Panzers? From General Marcks in St-Lô? From the 7th Army? In addition, he knew that in the event of an Allied landing on the

Hamilcars coming into land east of the Caen Canal. This was the largest glider available to the Allies and capable of carrying a light tank, artillery or other vehicles

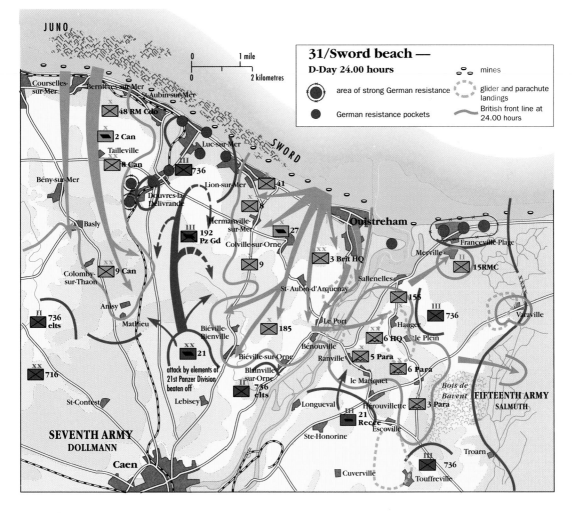

JUNO

Courselles-sur-Mer

Bernières-sur-Mer

St-Aubin-sur-Mer

48 RM Cdo

2 Can

Tailleville

8 Can

Luc-sur-Mer

Bény-sur-Mer

Douvres-la-Délivrande

736

Lion-sur-Mer

41

Basly

Hermanville-sur-Mer

8

192 Pz Gd

Colville-sur-Orne

27

9 Can

9

Colomby-sur-Thaon

St-Aubin-d'Arquenay

3 Brit HQ

Anisy

Mathieu

Biéville-Bienville

185

Le Port

736 elts

21

attack by elements of 21st Panzer Division beaten off

Biéville-sur-Orne

Blainville-sur-Orne

736 elts

Bénouville

Ranville

5 Para

716

Lebisey

Longueval

le Mariquet

3 Para

St-Contest

Hérouvillette

21 Recce

Escoville

Ste-Honorine

Ouistreham

Franceville-Plage

Merville

15RMC

Sallenelles

155

Hauger

736

Varaville

le Plein

6 HQ

6 Para

Bois de Bavent

FIFTEENTH ARMY

SALMUTH

Troarn

736

Cuverville

Touffreville

SEVENTH ARMY

DOLLMANN

Caen

31/Sword beach —

D-Day 24.00 hours

mines

area of strong German resistance

glider and parachute landings

German resistance pockets

British front line at 24.00 hours

0 — 1 mile
0 — 2 kilometres

SWORD

Orne, some of his infantry would at once come under the command of the 716th Division and his anti-aircraft battalion would be switched to the Caen coastal defences. In any event, no orders came. Eventually, at 6.30 a.m. on D-Day, after a night of agonizing frustration, he ordered some of his troops into action against the 6th Airborne.

Hour by hour, events brought the German commanders to their senses. At 9.00, Feuchtinger was told his 21st Panzers would in future respond to orders from General Marcks. Shortly after 10.00, orders came at last, nine hours after Feuchtinger himself knew of the first Allied attacks: he was to counterattack the invasion. This was not easy. His tanks would have to circle the bombed-out ruins of Caen, all the time savaged by fighter-bombers and clogged by lines of refugees.

And still no back-up. Hitler woke at 9.00 (10.00 British time) and listened to a briefing from his naval aide, Admiral Karl von Puttkamer, who passed on Jodl's news of an important landing. Hitler called in Jodl and Field Marshal Wilhelm Keitel, to whom he repeated again and again his certainty that this was not the main invasion. No one dared mention the reserves. Instead, Hitler told Jodl to start the bombardment of London with Germany's secret weapon, the long-range V-1 flying bombs.

Hitler remained apparently unconcerned. He cancelled his usual midday conference with his generals, driving off to see the new Hungarian premier at a castle near Salzburg. Then, after his customary vegetarian lunch, he at last issued the order to release the reserves. It would take another day for the reserves to get to the scene of action.

It was at Sword, the most easterly beach, and that closest to Caen, that the 21st Panzers would have their first and greatest impact. It would be, or should be, a momentous engagement, for Sword was the key to the whole Overlord operation. The beach was the gateway to Caen, on its plateau seven miles inland; and Caen was the gateway to the open country sweeping eastwards to the Seine, to Paris, and beyond.

The burden of this critical assault had been given to the 3rd British Infantry Division, and two commando brigades, the 1st and the 4th. It was the commandos who were to join up with the Canadians at Juno and also cut through to the hard-pressed 6th Airborne, still holding "Pegasus" bridge over the Caen Canal. Other units were to help take Caen, or at least "effectively mask" the town, in the carefully chosen words of Lt-General John Crocker, Commander of the 1st Corps, who well knew the chances of failure.

The assault forces, the 1st Battalion of the South Lancashire and 2nd East Yorkshire regiments, were led ashore by 25 DD's and landing craft carrying armored assault teams. Heavy sea and bad visibility almost brought catastrophe to the landing craft. Two of the tanks were rammed and sunk before the landing craft swung clear.

Among the first ashore were No. 4 Commando, in their green berets – they scorned helmets. Their commander, Lord Lovat, ordered his piper William Millin: "Give us 'Highland Laddie,' man!" Millin, waist-deep in water, sent the tune skirling down the beach, then continued piping the Commandos ashore, marching up and down the beach still playing, before running to the protection of the sea wall.

For many of those who survived, the first few minutes on Sword were the worst of the campaign. In places, the bodies were "stacked like cordwood." The impact was oddly uneven. Later, some recalled the landing being no worse then training. In any event, it was soon, over. In an hour the East Yorks, South Lancs and Commandos seized the beach, and cleared three exits. By then, there was little opposition except occasional sniper fire, and

British R.M. Commandos wade through waist-high seas after disembarking from their LST. The lone figure in the center of the picture is Lord Lovat

elated French civilians appeared to wave and shout a welcome. The mayor of Colleville even appeared right on the beach, wearing his regalia and brass helmet, to give the Allies an official greeting.

Meanwhile, the beach, shrinking by the minute under the incoming tide, turned to a melee as landing craft disgorged vehicles on to the narrowing strip of sand and gravel. Only at midday, with the obstacles and mines largely cleared and the tide retreating, did the congestion begin to ease.

Leading the march inland, the 1st South Lancs knew nothing of the chaos behind them. By 9.30 they were through Hermanville, a mile and a half on the road to Caen, clearing strongpoints and taking prisoners as they went. Now, almost within sight of Caen, they came up against the leading units of the 21st Panzers, three anti-tank guns set up outside Périers on a little ridge the British called Périers Ridge. The South Lancs dug in, and waited.

Why? It was an action that drew harsh judgements later. Perhaps if they had stormed ahead, they could have opened the way to Caen and the oppressed 6th Airborne across the Orne. They had their reasons: they were waiting for the King's Shropshire Light Infantry, who with the 65 tanks of the Staffordshire Yeomanry (all part of the 185th Brigade), were supposed to lead the mid-morning attack on Caen. But there was another, less rational explanation. The South Lancs had had no contact with the Germans since Dunkirk. They had trained at home, largely in defence. They and their commanders were imbued with all the tenacity of defenders, and little of the élan of assault troops. Having fulfilled their prime purpose of taking the beach, they seemed to run out of steam. So for three crucial hours, the South Lancs waited for the Shropshires, and the Shropshires back down the road near Hermanville waited for the tanks; and the tanks waited for the traffic jam on the beach to clear.

Eventually, the brigade commander decided he could afford to wait no longer. He ordered the Shropshires, to start forward on foot, hoping the tanks would catch up later. Under their commander, Lt-Col. F. J. Maurice, the Shropshires spread out and began to work forward through the ripe corn fields and hedge-lined roads. Around 2.00 p.m. some 20 Sherman tanks roared up behind them in time to assault Périers Ridge, and at last, the three German anti-tank guns fell silent.

Maurice pressed on. At 4.00 p.m., they were in Biéville, over half way to Caen. Three more miles to go. But a mile ahead, as yet unknown to them, lay the menace the British feared – 40 tanks of the 21st Panzers.

Now, at last, the German commanders knew exactly what was at stake. The tanks' commander, Colonel Hermann von Oppeln-Bronikowski, was met by both Feuchtinger and General Marcks, who had driven the 40 miles from St-Lô. This was the first real chance to stop the Allied advance. From that spot northwards, a corridor up to five miles wide ran between the forces landing at Juno and Sword. If the two Allied forces met up, all would be lost. But if Oppeln-Bronikowski's tanks could create a wall between the two, it might be possible to cut the invasion from its sea-based roots.

No sooner had the tanks set off, however, than they ran into Maurice's forces, and swung away west into woodland.

Two miles short of Caen the Shropshires came up against infantry dug in on a wooded ridge in front of Lebisey. They needed reinforcements, and there were none. There was nothing for it but to pull back, and wait at Biéville. Though they could not have guessed it then, this was as near as the British would get to Caen for weeks.

Behind them, the German tanks had hit the Périers Ridge, only to find it now well guarded by the British. Another seven tanks went up in flames. But to their left, the Germans were in the clear. Several tanks and a company of

British Commandos relax for a moment after their first action

infantry headed on northwards, unimpeded, striking the unguarded coast four miles further on at 8.00.

Back at their starting point, Feuchtinger despatched another 50 or so tanks to reinforce the advance force, but the tanks were brought to a sudden stop by an extraordinary sight. As they were slipping past Périers Ridge, a huge force of Allied planes – the largest glider-borne force in the whole war – droned low overhead in the evening sun. It consisted of scores of fighters protecting 250 transport planes, each towing a glider carrying infantry, artillery and light tanks to reinforce the 6th Airborne a few miles to the east. Swinging in low over the heads of the astonished Germans in a dense swarm, they would have been easy targets were it not for the Spitfires and Mustangs that dived down to rake the German tanks. As it was, only one of the gliders was brought down, though several were shot up on landing: one burning wreck briefly trapped its cargo, a tank, which escaped by bursting through the glider's flimsy sides.

Back towards Caen, Feuchtinger too saw the huge airborne force, saw that it was clearly unopposed by any German planes, and concluded that the gliders would be landing directly in the path of his tanks. To advance into that would be suicidal. He recalled his tanks.

For the Allies, the day was a great achievement – not yet a victory, not as great an achievement as had been planned, but given the bad weather and

A Sherman tank moves forward down a typical narrow bocage lane

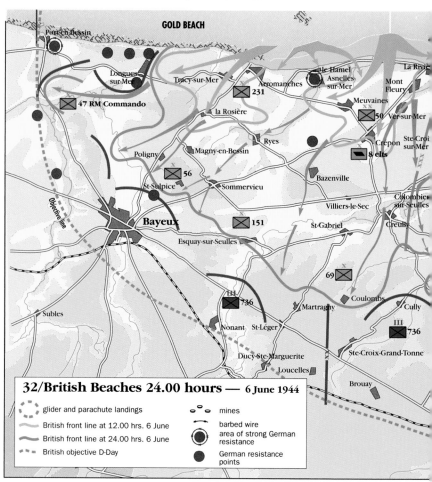

GOLD BEACH

32/British Beaches 24.00 hours — 6 June 1944

- glider and parachute landings
- British front line at 12.00 hrs. 6 June
- British front line at 24.00 hrs. 6 June
- British objective D-Day
- mines
- barbed wire
- area of strong German resistance
- German resistance points

the fearful risks, a great achievement nevertheless. The Atlantic Wall breached; the airborne forces still in place; the deception operation a brilliant success; the air totally cleared of enemy aircraft (the Allies had flown over 10,000 sorties, the Luftwaffe just 319, during which they shot down not a single Allied plane). The novel tactic of including armor in the landings had worked beautifully, and the "funnies" had proved them-selves invaluable. Over 150,000 men were on enemy soil, and there had been not a single major counterattack. Of the 10,000 or so casualties (the figures are still in doubt), some 2,500 men had died – a quarter of the number SHAEF had feared, which itself was half Churchill's nightmarish vision of 20,000 dead. No one knows how many Germans died that day – perhaps as few as 4,000, perhaps double that number, or more.

There was still much for the Allies to make up. Nowhere had the original objectives been achieved. The landings were running 8–12 hours behind schedule. The American seaborne forces still had to link with the British. There was still two gaps in Allied territory. Caen was still in enemy hands. At the end of the first day, there was no cause for complacency. The weather remained unsettled, and might yet forestall the flow of men, vehicles and supplies without which D-Day and the days following would all be in vain. If Caen held, if German tanks could rally fast enough, if German reinforcements could outnumber the forces pouring ashore, the invasion might yet fail.

A soldier of the 1st Battalion South Lancashire Regiment, 3rd Division watches from his front line position a Sherman tank reconnoitering no-man's land

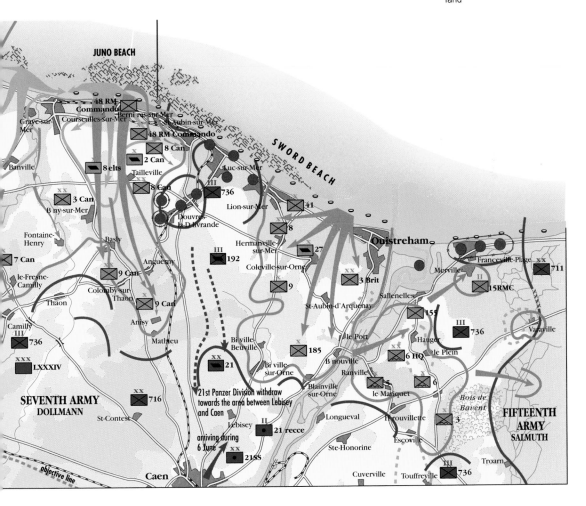

5 DEADLOCK AT CAEN

Aircraft bring in supplies to
U.S. Army troops fighting on
Utah Beach

For a day, perhaps, the door to the heart of Europe – Caen – stood ajar. In planning the invasion, and on D-Day itself, a rapid advance seemed all that was needed to throw it wide open. Instead, the opposite happened. German experience and fighting spirit slammed it shut. It would take weeks of battering, and several changes of strategy to open it again.

On June 7, the British 3rd Division's 185th Brigade failed in its attempt to continue the steady advance of the previous day through Lebisey. The 9th Brigade was stuck at Cambes. The 3rd Canadian Division, aiming at Carpiquet, came up against a formidable enemy, Colonel Kurt "Panzer" Meyer – 33, handsome, the very archetype of loyal Nazism – directing the tanks of the 12th SS Panzer Division from the top of the tower of Ardenne Abbey. His tank crews forced the Canadians to retreat two miles. The Germans were appalled that their advance was not more, while the Canadians were equally appalled at having to retreat at all. On the night of June 8, Meyer led tanks into action himself, on a motorcycle. This time, it was Meyer who retreated, with the loss of six Panthers. North of Caen, Juno and Sword joined forces. The line hardened. Neither side could advance.

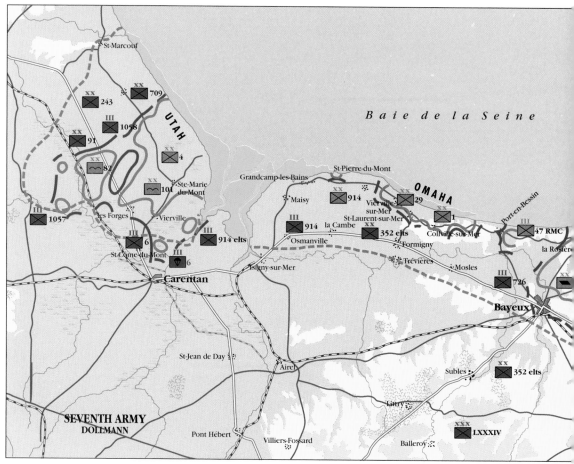

To the west of Caen, late on June 9, Panzer Lehr, with almost 3,000 tanks and vehicles, struggled into Tilly, south of Bayeux, after a gruelling 130-mile drive from Châteaudun, south of Chartres. Though well aware of the dangers, they had obeyed orders from the 7th Army's commander, General Friedrich Dollmann, to move during the day, with terrible results. They had been badly mauled by Allied planes, losing 130 trucks, five tanks and 84 other vehicles. But they had come through. Just short of Tilly on the Seulles River, they scattered across the sunken roads, thick hedges, stone walls and ruined houses west of Caen, well camouflaged and their approach tracks meticulously cleared. These were elite troops, led by Lt-General Fritz Bayerlein, once Rommel's chief-of-staff in Africa.

This pretty bocage country, "La Suisse Normande," with its hills, streams, orchards and little patchwork fields of cowslips and buttercups, was good to defend and hellish to attack. The solid earthen walls, dense old hedges and woods provided wonderful cover for snipers, mortar crews and gunners with the superbly effective 88's, while tight-packed villages acted as fortified strongpoints. Here, armor, overwhelming numbers, bombers and artillery could not substitute for the small group, led with skill and determination, on the move, creeping, rushing, hiding, firing. Tanks in a narrow lane – as the Allied forces often had to be – were like skittles in a bowling alley. Their commanders could not see over the hedges; they could not swing their guns; they couldn't turn; they couldn't escape if attacked. Off the roads – and the Allies were advancing across the grain of the countryside and its roads – the

Young German prisoners anxiously await their fate just behind the front line

33/Allied Bridgehead–

24.00 hours 6th June

——— Allied front line

〜〜〜 German positions

- - - - Allied objective line for end of D-Day "D + 1"

| 0 | | 10 miles |
| 0 | | 15 kms |

GOLD JUNO

Romanches Crépon Bernières-sur-Mer St-Aubin-sur-Mer
Banville Courselles-sur-Mer Luc-sur-Mer
XX 50 Bény-sur-Mer Lion-sur-Mer Houlgate
Creully XX 51 Basly XX 736 elts SWORD Ouistreham Franceville-Plage Cabourg
St-Léger Thaon XX 736 XX 5 Varaville XX 736 elts
Bretteville l'Orgueilleuse XX 6 Hérouvillette
St-Manvieu Carpiquet XX 716 XX 21 Escoville FIFTEENTH ARMY SALMUTH
Caen
XXX ISS
XX 12SS

Allied Troop Landing Figures – By End of D-Day – 6 June 1944

U.S. Sector	U.K. & Can. Sector
Utah Beach 23,250	Gold Beach 24,970
Omaha Beach 34,250	Juno Beach 21,400
	Sword Beach 28,845
Airborne	
15,500	7,900
TOTALS (approximately)	
73,000	83,115

TOTAL ALLIED TROOPS LANDED IN FRANCE 156,000 plus

barriers made every field a castle. Every open space meant possible exposure to a machine gun or mortar, every hiding place was a potential trap.

To break the deadlock, Montgomery decided to use two divisions he knew well from the Eighth Army in North Africa – the 51st Highland Division and 7th Armoured, the "Desert Rats." Neither had been part of the D-Day assault. Both had just landed, and eased their way clear of the chaos on the beaches. Together they would encircle Caen, the Highlanders passing through 6th Airborne to the north, the Desert Rats to the south, from Tilly to Villers-Bocage and beyond. Montgomery's plan called for the pincer to be snapped shut by the British 1st Airborne Division, but the air drop was vetoed by Air Vice Marshal Sir Trafford Leigh-Mallory. Montgomery was furious, but was unable to overturn the veto.

That attack, finally launched on June 10, misfired completely. Though Panzer Group West's HQ, blatantly uncamouflaged in an orchard, was destroyed by an air raid the previous day, local forces were enough to stop the Highlanders within hours. The cost on both sides was appalling. When the 5th Battalion of the Black Watch advanced towards Bréville, they sustained 200 casualties. The 12th Battalion of the Paras took the village next day at terrible cost. Of 160 men involved, only 19 came through un-scathed. The 546 defenders were reduced to 146. In all sectors, the con-

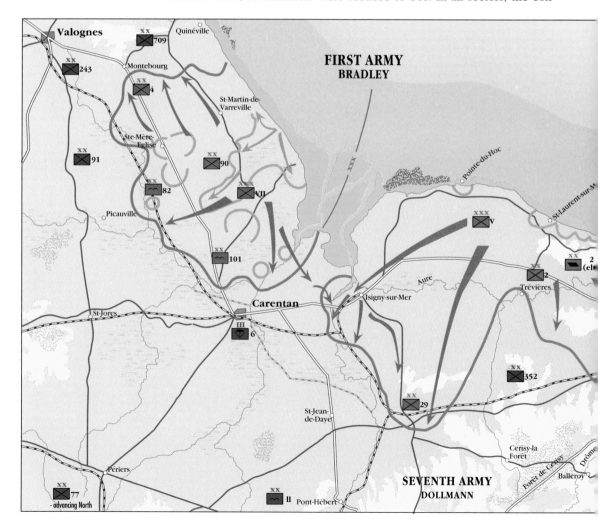

tinuous bombardment shredded nerves and equipment alike. Tanks would edge forward, with infantry huddled up to them for protection, only to find the fire too intense, and reverse, often over their own wounded. Men on both sides sank into depression and exhaustion. But the Germans held fast.

British troops inspect a "knocked-out" Panzer Mk.IV

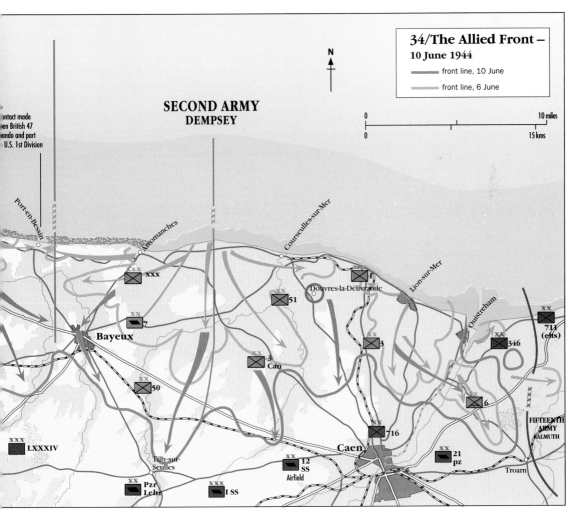

34/The Allied Front –
10 June 1944

front line, 10 June
front line, 6 June

0   10 miles
0   15 kms

SECOND ARMY
DEMPSEY

N

ontact made
en British 47
ando and part
U.S. 1st Division

Port-en-Bessin

Arromanches

Courseulles-sur-Mer

Lion-sur-Mer

Ouistreham

XXX

XXX

XXX

Douvres-la-Délivrande

1

XX 51

XX 7

XX 3

XX 711 (elts)

Bayeux

XX 346

XX 3 Can

XX 50

XX 6

XX 716

FIFTEENTH ARMY SALMUTH

XXX LXXXIV

Caen

XX 21 pz

Troarn

Tilly-sur-Seulles

XX 12 SS

Airfield

XX Pzr Lehr

XXX I SS

A Panzer Mk.IV of the 12th SS Panzer Division with the tank commander and the loader, west of Caen, in June 1944

On the other side of Caen, the 50th Division and the Desert Rats were equally unsuccessful. The 50th Division's commander ordered the 6th Battalion of the Green Howards to probe a possible gap in the German lines between Cristot and Tilly. The nine Sherman tanks advanced too fast, speeding ahead through orchards and cornfields, failing to spot well-hidden grenadiers of the 12th SS Panzers. When the tanks were past, the Germans mowed down the Green Howards and opened up on the tanks from the rear. After a bloody exchange, the British retreated. Only two of the tanks escaped. The Green Howards lost 24 officers and 250 men.

The 7th Armoured's commander, General George "Bobby" Erskine, saw a second chance: a hole in the German's front line between Caumont and the hilltop town of Villers-Bocage, a key to high ground to the south to the valley of the Odon River, and to Caen itself. Dempsey and the 30th Corps commander, Lt-General G.C. Bucknall, agreed, and the order was given to start an action that turned into one of the most controversial engagements of the whole campaign. Even the order itself had controversy conferred upon it by

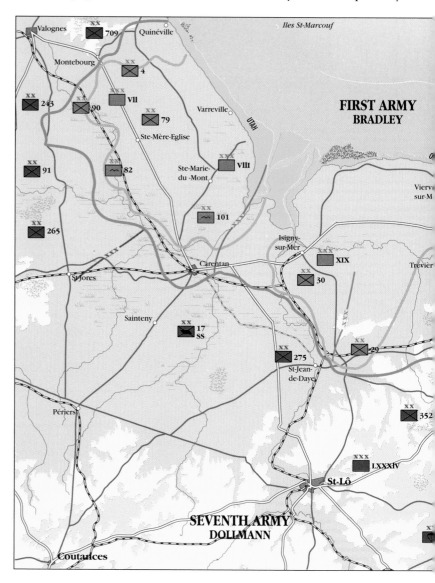

subsequent events. The idea was sound but it took 24 hours to become a reality. Those 24 hours were to prove vital.

The leading units – from 22nd Armoured Brigade – spent the night of June 12 just outside Caumont, five miles from Villers-Bocage, and sped on into it the next morning, leading a column of infantry in half-tracks. Astonishingly, there was no resistance, and the locals turned out to welcome their liberators. The brigade commander, Brigadier Robert Hinde – nicknamed "Looney" for his fearlessness – ordered tanks to escort half-tracks eastward towards a high point designated 213, a couple of miles along the wooded road that led towards Caen.

For a few minutes all was quiet. But up ahead lay five tanks of 101st Heavy SS-Tank Battalion, four of them 56-ton Tigers, the fifth a Mk.IV. They had precisely the same task as the British – to occupy Point 213. The British vehicles were sitting ducks, trapped in the narrow road, hemmed in by high hedges and banks. Led by Lieutenant Michael Wittmann, who had won a reputation on the Eastern Front as Germany's greatest Panzer "ace," the

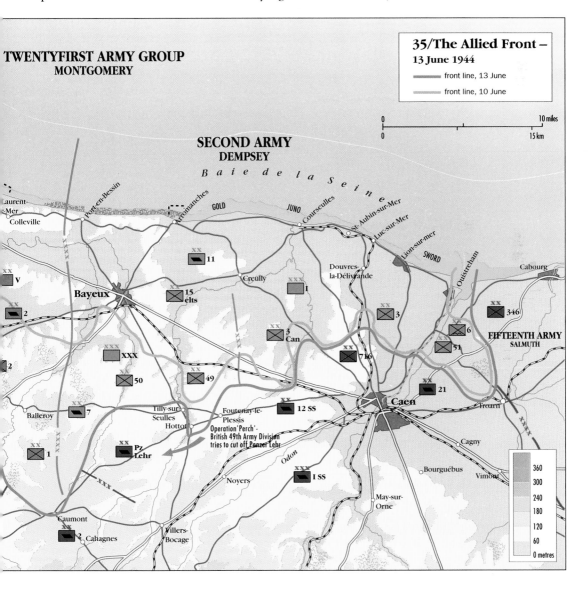

German Tigers had left Beauvais four days before, travelling only by night. Now Wittmann, hidden in woods overlooking Point 213, watched stationary British vehicles and the men stretching their legs with some surprise.

His gunner said: "They're acting as if they've won the war already."

"We're going to prove them wrong," said Wittmann.

The incident that followed, told and retold in many different versions, has only recently been analyzed in detail. Wittmann decided to by-pass the British column and go for its base, Villiers-Bocage itself. Heading downhill into the village, he attacked four Cromwells lined up in the road. His 88 knocked out three. The fourth reversed out of sight into a garden, and then as Wittmann rumbled on downhill, followed. After exchanging a few shots with other British tanks, Wittmann turned, took two ineffective hits from the Cromwell stalking him, knocked it out, accelerated out of the village off the road, and only then attacked the isolated British column, systematically reducing its Fireflies, trucks, Bren-gun carriers and half-tracks to burning wrecks. Meanwhile, in the village, four other Cromwells had grouped in the square in case Wittmann returned. This he did, with another Tiger and the Mark .IV – and ran right into the trap. The British knocked out the three German tanks with shots to the flanks and rear. Wittmann escaped on foot, along with his crew. He was credited with 138 "kills" in all before he himself was killed two months later.

The British armor in Villers-Bocage was still dangerously exposed and over

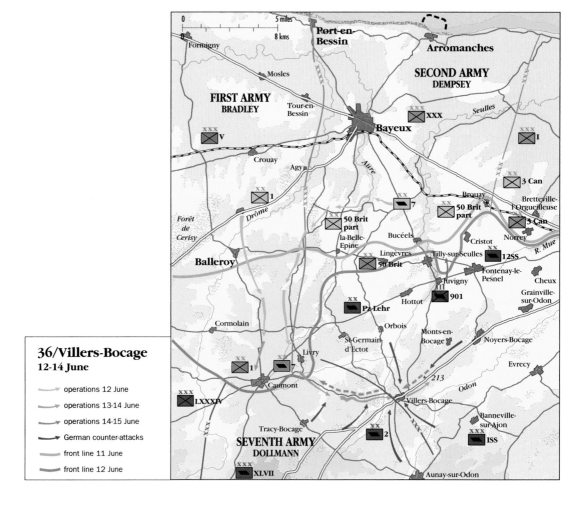

36/Villers-Bocage
12-14 June

→ operations 12 June
→ operations 13-14 June
→ operations 14-15 June
→ German counter-attacks
— front line 11 June
— front line 12 June

the next two days pulled right back, under cover of an American artillery barrage and an RAF bombing raid that wrecked Villers-Bocage. The British had lost 25 tanks and 28 armored vehicles and did not renew the attack. The gap in the German lines closed.

All in all, it was a disastrous outcome for which all the senior commanders have been blamed for a catalogue of errors: slowness in decision making, too many risks taken, lack of plan, failure to commit reinforcements. There is justice in much of this. There was a gap in the German lines until the arrival of the 2nd Panzer, and the Germans were surprised that it was not better exploited. Later, both Erskine and Bucknall (who came in for the greatest criticism) were fired.

This was not what Montgomery had planned. Despite the weather, the invasion had gone well. The Germans had been successfully deceived and their response had been even slower than expected. And yet the advance had been stopped. The setback also severely undermined the reputation the Desert Rats had won in North Africa. The 7th Armoured had proven particularly susceptible to conditions in the bocage. Used to swift open warfare in the desert, they had retrained for Overlord in the broad fenlands and heaths of Norfolk. Accustomed to engaging at 800 yards or more, they were now suddenly subjected to anti-tank guns at 50 yards, even to boarding parties leaping on their tank-hulls from hedgerows. At the time Dempsey was restrained, but in a post-war interview he revealed his anger and disappointment: "The 7th Armoured Division was living on its reputation and the whole handling of that battle was a disgrace." As Dempsey saw it, Caen could now be taken only by a huge set piece assault for which the Allies did not yet have the men or equipment. A campaign which should have been measured in days would now take weeks and cost hundreds of lives.

The only Allied advantage gained by the Villers-Bocage debacle was that the confrontation drew in German armor which might otherwise have been rushed to the defence of Cherbourg. This was perforce the policy Montgomery had now to favor, since his original plan to preserve movement and break out into open tank country beyond Caen had dissolved. It was a flawed policy, with ever higher stakes. The longer the wait, the greater the

Lieutenant Michael Wittmann, the famous tank commander, sitting on his Tiger tank in Normandy, 1944

Sherman tanks driving south through the countryside near Caumont

opposition, the harder the final battle, and the greater the risks of the whole advance being held up until – and perhaps through – winter. This was a hideous scenario, threatening something more reminiscent of the Western Front of World War One than the sweeping campaign of Monty's plan.

Rommel spent the first few days after D-Day driving from unit to unit, learning, inspiring, demanding. He still believed there would be a second invasion elsewhere, and refused to draw in reserves from the 15th Army in the Pas de Calais. With all the Seine bridges down, any reinforcements from there would have to go by rail and road via Paris, an epic journey impossible to reverse once the expected invasion of Pas de Calais came. With the forces at hand he had successfully slowed the Allied advance, but there was a limit to such frantic improvisation. Every counter-move was frustrated by shattered communications, broken railway lines, fuel shortages, lack of ammunition and Allied air attacks. All he could hope for was a little more time. As he bitterly told OKW on June 12: "The enemy has complete command of the air and cuts off by day almost all traffic on roads or byways or in open country."

For example: on D-Day, OKW had ordered up several units from Brittany and the 2nd SS Panzer Division ("Das Reich") from Toulouse. Of the local units few had motor transport. They were reduced to horse-drawn carts, bicycles and foot-slogging. One regiment coming from Nantes by train had the rear wagons, which contained their horses, severed in an American air strike and had to continue on foot. The 2nd SS Panzer in Toulouse took 11 days simply to load up all their armor. It took another two weeks of being bombed, strafed and harrassed by the Resistance before all of them could cover the 450 miles to St-Lô.

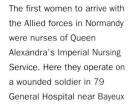

The first women to arrive with the Allied forces in Normandy were nurses of Queen Alexandra's Imperial Nursing Service. Here they operate on a wounded soldier in 79 General Hospital near Bayeux

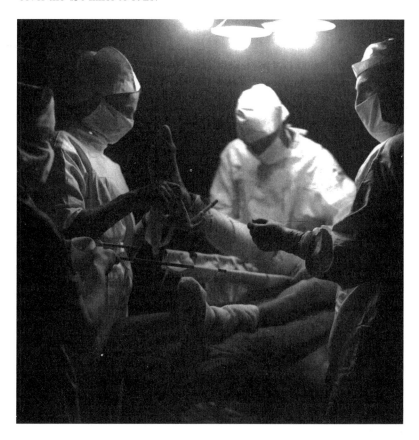

Monsieur Doisy Marcel, a builder by trade, shows a British sergeant how he concealed stolen German ammunition in paving stones

Within days a new sense of realism spread gloom through the German commanders. Since there was a total intelligence vacuum – no air reconnaissance, no agents' reports, no way to crack Allied radio codes – no one had any idea what the Allies would do. One thing was clear: the advance in Normandy was unstoppable. There would be no breakthrough to the sea. Sepp Dietrich, the old commander of the I Panzer Corps, told Rommel the line would hold for no more than three weeks. When Rommel ordered him to attack, he exploded: "With what? We need another eight or ten divisions in the next few days or we are finished." Rommel became desperate. In the battle for Tilly and Villers-Bocage up to June 25, Panzer Lehr lost 160 officers, 5,400 men and two thirds of its 190 tanks. The line had held, but at what cost? "There's simply no answer to it," he wrote to his wife. "It will all be over very quickly."

The truth was that there was little Rommel could do to affect the course of the war. Even if he had been present on D-Day itself, even if he had galvanized the tanks into action sooner, the invasion would not have been stopped and its final outcome not altered. The only course open to him was progressive and hard-fought retreat. That way, at least, the Germans would have been clear of Allied naval gunfire. If retreat had been an option, reserves could have been brought in from southern France and the Pas de Calais.

But retreat was not an option. On June 10 Hitler ordered: "There can be no question of fighting a rearguard action. Every man will fight and fall where he stands."

Not that the German plight was obvious to the Americans. Fighting clear of their two bridgeheads, the Americans from Utah found the going harder and those from Omaha easier than the landings had led them to expect. The

82nd, after fighting off a counterattack, were revived by glider-borne reinforcements and by German uncertainty – the German High Command had been confused by a landing of dummy parachutists near St-Lô. From Omaha, V Corps' 29th Division worked westward to relieve the Rangers on Pointe du Hoc and eastwards to link up with the British from Gold, while the 1st and 2nd Divisions advanced south to Carentan, which in German hands would keep troops from the two American beaches wedged apart. On June 11 the 101st Airborne fought their way into the little town and the Germans withdrew.

Trying to whip up enough tanks and troops to hold the line, General Marcks had set off to a hill near Caumont when his car was attacked by Allied fighters. He tried to take cover but he was slowed by his wooden leg and died in the hail of bullets. Caumont fell and the Allied line took another step southwards. The next day after the fall of Carentan, the American 2nd Armored and 101st Airborne linked up across a great expanse of wet lowlands with troops from Omaha. The two American beachheads were at last joined.

Once that link had been made, the principal task of the Americans – Major-General J. Lawton Collins' VII Corps – was to secure the Cotentin Peninsula, in particular its lynch-pin, Cherbourg, without which the Allies would have

American soldiers make best use of cover in the advance towards Avranches

no major port. For that to happen successfully and fast, the whole peninsula had to be cut in order to shield the troops advancing northwards from German reinforcements from the south. "Lightnin' Joe" Collins, who sprang from inter-war limbo to win a quick reputation for ruthlessness and drive in the jungles of Guadalcanal, was just the man to mastermind such a rapid advance.

The cross-country assault by the 9th Division and some of the 82nd proved relatively easy. The country was densely-matted bocage, all small fields and stout hedges, but Collins sliced forward along a narrow front, quickly dealing with the isolated pockets of Germans. Since the higher quality German troops and armor were already committed to the defence of Caen, most of the German tanks in the Cotentin were captured French armor and there was little hope of cutting off Collins's advance. Instead, Collins cut clean through the Germans.

A northern group under Major-General Karl von Schlieben fell back towards Cherbourg – to Hitler's fury. "Very well then!" he shouted when he heard the news. "If they won't hold there" – indicating the old front on a map with a red pencil – "then there!" and he slashed a line across the Cotentin south of Cherbourg. It was a random and foolish order, for to hold that line would mean scattering the remaining troops along a wide front

instead of concentrating them where they were most needed – the defences of Cherbourg.

When the Americans reached the coast early on June 18, the 9th Division turned south to extend the coastal bridgehead, and north, rolling up the peninsula in conjunction with two other divisions already in place behind them to take Cherbourg.

Meanwhile, at the beaches, the landings continued with all possible speed. Speed was vital, for petrol, ammunition and supplies were being eaten up at a phenomenal rate which grew greater as more men and equipment landed. Each G.I. needed 30 pounds of supplies a day in food, ammunition and equipment. Then there were the vehicles themselves, which all needed fuel, ammunition and spares. Combined, the beaches would receive 2,500 vehicles a day, which meant 3,000 tons of supplies immediately, rising to 26,000 tons over the next two weeks.

Troops build a caliper wall and bridge to connect with a distant pier

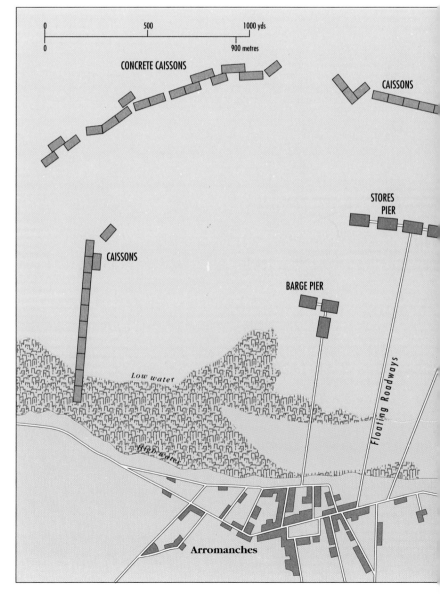

To achieve this, the artificial harbors were vital. A first convoy of 45 ships arrived the day after D-Day, followed every day by further convoys of tugs towing the caissons, pierheads and roadways that would form the new harbors – an American one off St-Laurent and a British one off Arromanches. They were staggering creations, with gangling four-mile breakwaters making two huge rectangles, their sides two miles apart and the outer walls a mile out to sea. The massive 6,000-ton caissons, which formed the outer breakwaters, had to be placed accurately along with sunken blockships (code-named Gooseberries) to form sea walls. These barriers protected piers from which ran cantilevered "Whale" roadways borne on pontoons, seven miles in all, so that trucks could pass to and fro whatever the state of the tide or weather.

There was little the Germans did or could do to hamper the build-up. Of the 42 U-boats in French coastal ports, 12 were sunk and none even got through to the invasion route until the end of June. There were destroyers in

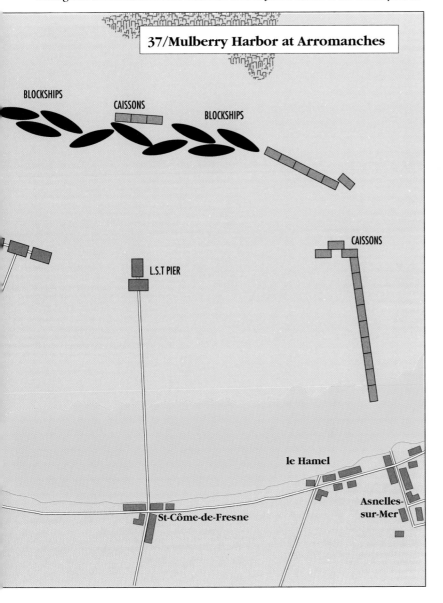

37/Mulberry Harbor at Arromanches

BLOCKSHIPS

CAISSONS

BLOCKSHIPS

CAISSONS

L.S.T PIER

le Hamel

Asnelles-sur-Mer

St-Côme-de-Fresne

St-Nazaire and torpedo-boats in Le Havre and Cherbourg, but all were blocked by patrols. A new mine, the "oyster," which was detonated by a change in water pressure as a vessel passed, caused some concern until the Allies discovered that it was possible to go slowly enough to avoid detonation. Other types of mine were cleared by minesweepers each day.

By mid-June all at last was beginning to go well for the Allies. On June 17, 34,000 troops and 25,000 tons of stores were landed, bringing the Allied strength up to 20 divisions – about 500,000 men – ahead at last of the Germans' 18 badly degraded divisions.

Rommel and Rundstedt were now certain there could be no defence without a new strategy. Hitler, too, was pinning his hopes on a new strategy – the V-1s, which were to pound London into abject surrender. Originally the attacks were due to start on June 12. About 12,000 of the flying bombs had been made but they had been dispersed to protect them against bombs and the rail links that would carry them to their launch-sites were broken. On June 12 only seven of the 64 sites were working. Ten bombs were launched, only one of which reached London. Three days later, 244 bombs took off. They were indeed shocking to Londoners, but defences proved adequate. Only 2,420 "doodle-bugs" ever reached London, causing some 6,000 deaths (another 4,300 crashed or were destroyed en route). In fact, the whole

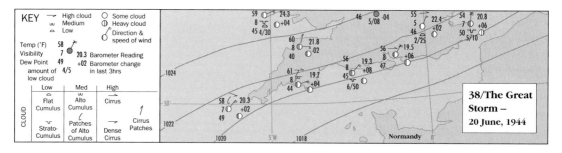

KEY

High cloud — Some cloud O
Medium ω — Heavy cloud ◑
Low ◠ — Direction & speed of wind

Temp (°F) 58
Visibility 7 — 20.3 Barometer Reading
Dew Point 49 — +02 Barometer change in last 3hrs
amount of 4/5 low cloud

CLOUD	Low	Med	High
	Flat Cumulus	Alto Cumulus	Cirrus
	Strato-Cumulus	Patches of Alto Cumulus	Dense Cirrus / Cirrus Patches

38/The Great Storm – 20 June, 1944

By mid-July 1944, the mighty supply organization the Allied planners had envisaged was a reality. Here landing craft are disgorging reinforcements and supplies

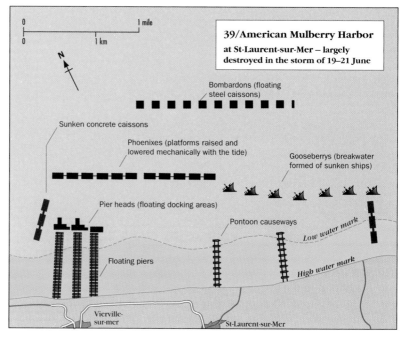

39/American Mulberry Harbor at St-Laurent-sur-Mer – largely destroyed in the storm of 19–21 June

Bombardons (floating steel caissons)

Sunken concrete caissons

Phoenixes (platforms raised and lowered mechanically with the tide)

Gooseberrys (breakwater formed of sunken ships)

Pier heads (floating docking areas)

Pontoon causeways

Low water mark

Floating piers

High water mark

Vierville-sur-mer

St-Laurent-sur-Mer

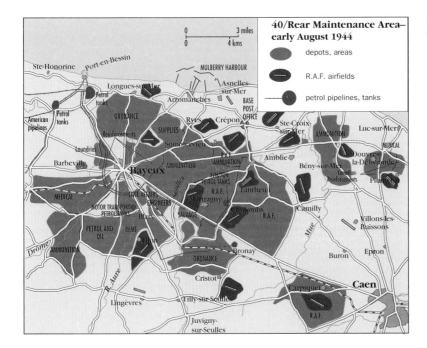

operation worked as much against the Germans as for them: the bombing raids against the launch sites served to confirm in German minds the fallacy that a second invasion in the Pas de Calais was imminent.

On June 17 Hitler could still delude himself that the V-1s would do their intended job. On that day he at last responded to the increasingly dire reports from Rundstedt and Rommel by coming to Margival, near Soissons, 50 miles north east of Paris. Here was the bombproof command post from which he had intended to direct the invasion of England.

Rommel pointed out that he was engaged in a hopeless struggle, given the enemy's command of sea, air and land. The only course was to pull back beyond the range of naval gunfire and retrench. Only then could the armor be freed to throw back any attempted breakthrough. Hitler, apparently accepting what Rommel said, spoke of other things through lunch, over-riding discussion. Later, when Rommel suggested ending the war now, Hitler became angry, trying to cut Rommel off and asserting that the V-1 attacks would be decisive and finally telling him in effect to mind his own business. He, Hitler, would decide the course of the war.

Rommel and Rundstedt left having wrung from Hitler a promise to visit Army Group B headquarters two days later. That grudging promise was killed off by a strange irony: a rogue V-1 circled back and landed right on the bunker. No one was hurt, but Hitler was so shocked that he cancelled his trip and sped back to the safety of Berchtesgaden, fuming at the defeatism of his generals.

It was no new offensive that threatened the Allied advance, but something far more potent. On the night of June 19 the Allied commanders' greatest fear was realized. In the early hours of June 20, just when tugs were in mid-Channel with another 2.5 miles of roadway for the Mulberries, a storm blew up, a "gale such as had not been known in the Channel in Summer for eighty years." All the roadway vanished under the waves. Other convoys turned back. By early afternoon the breakers were 8 feet high. The storm lasted for three days during which hardly anything could be brought across, moored or landed. About 140,000 tons of supplies went down and 800 ships were either lost or beached – far greater losses than anything the Germans had been able to mete out.

Some 500 landing craft sheltered inside the Arromanches Mulberry, which survived well enough. But the American harbor, which was more exposed, was wrecked beyond repair. Two of the blockships broke their backs, while 25 of the 35 caissons were tossed aside. Waves tore the piers and roadways apart more effectively than enemy fire.

The Allied build-up slowed catastrophically. After the storm only a fifth of the planned quantities of men and supplies could be landed. The Americans were left with just two days of ammunition and the British were three full divisions short. It was all the more vital to secure Cherbourg.

Landwards, Cherbourg was defended by three ridge lines – undermanned, since to fulfill Hitler's ludicrous order von Schlieben had scattered a third of his 21,000 troops outside the town's defence perimeter. His forces were as he said frankly "inferior." A fifth of them were Russians or Poles. It had taken all their spirit and strength just to retreat. They had few supplies, and little chance of any more. All they could do was sit inside their massive concrete bunkers and pour out machine-gun fire.

A stupefying bombardment signalled the final assault on June 22. The American advance demanded steady, dogged, dangerous steps from strong-point to strongpoint, with bombers and artillery forcing the defenders back into the concrete defences upon which the infantry closed in with explosives and phosphorous grenades. Progress was slow, but inexorable, house-to-house, through Cherbourg to its heart, Fort du Roule, and the network of tunnels and bunkers that shielded the thousands of troops and personnel.

After four days von Schlieben was captured. Resistance ended two days later. In their relief the men of the 9th Division celebrated with captured brandy, wine and champagne. Their commander, General Manton Eddy, despaired of controlling them. "Okay," he conceded, "everybody take 24 hours and get drunk." The liquor of Cherbourg, loaded into captured vehicles, would go with VII Corps across Europe. Those who followed Eddy's advice had reason to regret it when on June 28 they began a 12-mile march westward to secure the last German outpost on Cap de la Hague, which finally fell on June 30.

Meanwhile, Cherbourg itself remained a problem. Already the campaign was running days behind schedule. Now the Allies discovered with consternation that the harbor had been the target of thorough-going demolition.

The remains of the American Mulberry harbor at St-Laurent after the storms of 19–21 June. This harbor was more exposed than the British harbor at Arromanches and was not rebuilt

Supposedly, the port was to process 150,000 tons of stores by late July. In fact, by then it would handle little over ten percent of that figure and would not be fully operational for another month.

When Monty again – for the third time – decided to take Caen, he planned to have a more massive force at his disposal: three corps, spearheaded by VIII Corps, with 60,000 men, 600 tanks, 700 guns then landing under the command of Monty's old friend, Lt-General Sir Richard O'Connor, who had led the first British campaign in the western desert and had then spent two years in a POW camp in Italy from which he made a daring escape. The operation, codenamed Epsom, was intended to be a hook around Caen to the south, on a four-mile front to the west of Carpiquet. This semi-encirclement would open the way to the plain beyond Caen, isolate Caen itself, and draw in German armor from further west, weakening the line around St-Lô and making possible an American breakthrough there. Time

Lt-General Karl von Schlieben, commander of the Cherbourg garrison, surrenders on 27 June

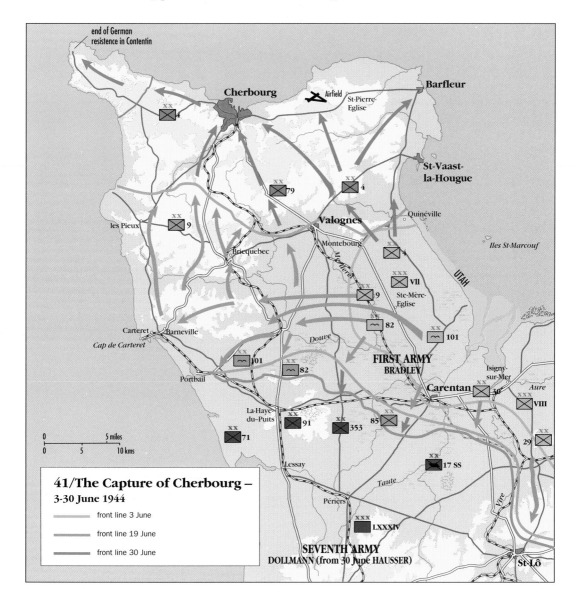

end of German resistence in Contentin

Cherbourg

Airfield St-Pierre-Eglise

Barfleur

XX 4

St-Vaast-la-Hougue

XX 79

XX 4

Quinéville

les Pieux

XX 9

Valognes

Montebourg

Iles St-Marcouf

Briequebec

XXX 4

UTAH

XXX VII

XX 9

Ste-Mère-Eglise

Carteret   Barneville

Douve

~ 82

XX ~ 101

Cap de Carteret

XX ~ 101

XX ~ 82

FIRST ARMY
BRADLEY

Isigny-sur-Mer

Portbail

Carentan XX 30

Aure

XXX VIII

La-Haye-du-Puits

XX 91

XX 353

XX 85

0   5 miles
0   5   10 kms

XX 71

XX 29

Lessay

XX 17 SS

Taute

Périers

Vire

41/The Capture of Cherbourg –
3-30 June 1944

front line 3 June

front line 19 June

front line 30 June

XXX LXXXIV

SEVENTH ARMY
DOLLMANN (from 30 June HAUSSER)

St-Lô

was of the essence. German tank reinforcements were on their way to Caen. As Montgomery told his senior officers: "We have now reached the showdown stage."

Again plans misfired. The assault, originally planned for June 23, was set back two days by the Channel storm – half of O'Connor's force was held back by the weather, allowing German opposition to harden. The 12th SS Panzer, elements of 21st Panzer and Panzer Lehr, had 228 tanks and assault guns and 150 88mm guns screening Caen and its surroundings on a 15-mile-wide front.

When Epsom opened, the 15th (Scottish) Division, with its many famous regiments – among them the Cameronians and the Gordon Highlanders – was

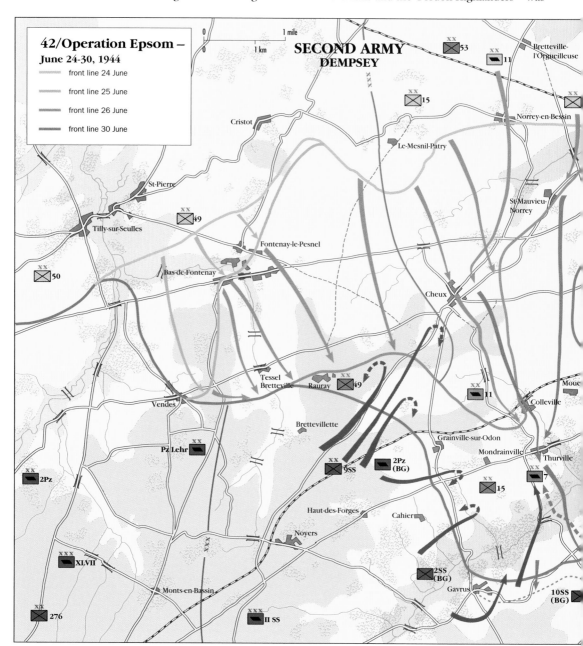

42/Operation Epsom –
June 24-30, 1944

front line 24 June
front line 25 June
front line 26 June
front line 30 June

SECOND ARMY
DEMPSEY

supposed to advance five miles, take bridges over the Odon, then hold them while tanks swept on ahead to the Orne. But the campaign no sooner opened than it slowed. It was raining. Under lowering skies there could be virtually no aircraft support. British infantry staggered to a halt as German fire poured in from hedges and houses. The day ended in a morass and with all units short of their objectives.

The next day, after holding off a counterattack, the British managed to reach the Odon and take a bridge. On June 28 the tanks of the 11th Armoured roared across the Odon River and up to a hill labelled 112 overlooking the road and leading away from Caen, five miles to the north east. In the 7th Army HQ, General Dollmann, who had just heard news of the

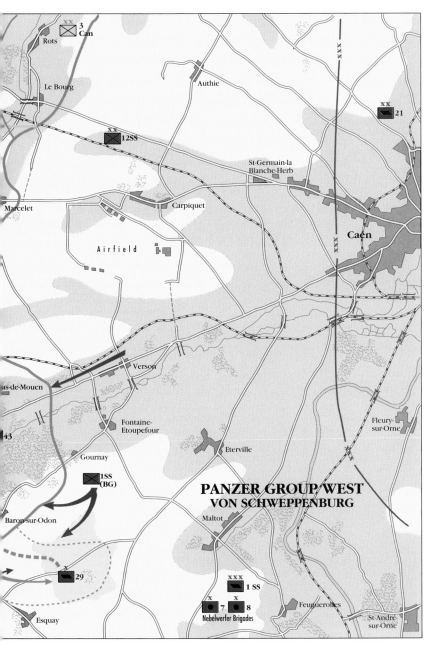

British mine clearance teams alerting the Allied troops and locals alike to the remaining danger of German mines

fall of Cherbourg, panicked. He ordered a counterattack by the II SS Panzer Corps, and then committed suicide by taking poison. With no one to countermand his last ill-conceived order, the German Panzers went ahead with their counterattack against Hill 112, for which they were not in the least prepared. They were beaten off.

Dempsey, however, was told of an intercepted German order revealing that there would be a further German assault. Thinking the British flanks too exposed, he ordered O'Connor to pull the tanks back across the Odon. The next day the Germans retook Hill 112.

To continue the fight in this Somme-like struggle for a muddy no-man's-land would rapidly lead to horrendous losses. At one point, the Odon was completely blocked by corpses. In the 15th Division's infantry units, casualties were running at 50 percent. This was a price Montgomery could not contemplate paying. On June 30 he ordered an end to Epsom – 4,000 men had died or been wounded in vain.

It was the second disastrous setback in two weeks. Several Allied commanders began to suspect that the invasion and breakout plan had been flawed from the beginning.

It might have been a matter of leadership. Certainly, Montgomery had his faults. Instead of accepting a degree of responsibility, he preserved a facade of omniscience, claiming that what was not achieved was not important. The deadlock at Caen became part of his grand scheme : "I never once had cause or reason to alter my master plan," he wrote in his memoirs. Clearly his plans had changed. His strategy was now in effect not to seize Caen but to besiege it, using it as an anchor or "hinge" for a breakthrough to the west. His refusal to acknowledge the change drew increasingly harsh criticism from his colleagues. Later, many were damning in their condemnation. One of the Overlord planners, Captain J. Hughes-Hallett, put it about as bluntly as anyone could: "Monty's talk of his original intention to hinge on Caen was absolute balls."

But to those below him, Monty's conceit appeared more as an undentable self-confidence, which restored morale while protecting him from disapproval. A lieutenant in the Buffs said: "It seemed an absolute deadlock.

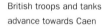

British troops and tanks advance towards Caen

A British ammunition lorry
explodes, hit by German
mortar fire

There was some effect on morale, and places got a bad name, like Caumont. But when Montgomery passed us one day in his staff car all my crew stood up in the tank and cheered."

What Montgomery could not do at this stage was upgrade the quality of the equipment. Nor could he inject the right qualitites, where these were lacking, into his junior officers and men – and if not into the British then certainly not into the Americans. Nor could he undermine the fighting spirit of the Germans. The deadlock had highlighted an alarming difference in the fighting effectiveness of Allied and German troops – not a universal difference, for there were countless examples of astonishing skill and courage amongst Allied commanders and men and many of instant and willing surrender by Germans, but striking enough to be remarked at the time and a matter of controversy since.

One part of the problem lay in organization. In the simplest terms, the German army was a product of war, the British army was a product of class and the American army a product of industry. The American war machine had huge redundancies. At the time of the Normandy landings, combat troops formed 54 percent of the German army and 38 per cent of the American army. In actual combat divisions, the difference was even more marked: 44 percent against 20 percent. Proportionally, in organizational terms, the Germans were between about 1.5 and 2 times as efficient, though that efficiency could not possibly prevail against America's overwhelming manpower and industrial capacity.

A second part of the problem was the difference in quality between weapons. The German machine guns – MG (Maschinengewehr, "machine gun") 34s and 42s – could pour out 900 and 1,200 rounds a minute respectively, roughly twice the rate of fire of the Bren gun and four times that of the Vickers. The Germans had equivalent advantages in grenades, small arms, mortars and bazookas. The 88mm anti-aircraft gun when turned on tanks or infantry had a devastating effect.

German Tigers and Panthers constantly showed themselves more than a match for the Allies' Shermans, Churchills and Cromwells, a fact that was consistently fudged by the government in London. The 56-ton Tigers were formidable vehicles and the 70-ton "King Tigers," then beginning production, would have been even more so. A 75mm shell from a Sherman simply bounced off a Tiger's 100mm frontal armor, whereas a Tiger's 88mm gun could "brew up" Shermans – which had an unnerving propensity to catch fire – at a range of two miles. The 50-ton Panther, with its speed, sloping armor and high-velocity 75mm gun, was designed to counter the superb Russian T-34. Both had their weaknesses, notably a slow-turning turret, so that the smaller Allied tanks could hope to get in quick shots to flank or rear before the German machines could aim and fire. But in good hands they could be counted on to outgun the Allied armor.

There were many good hands. For a force that was outnumbered, out-flown and facing defeat on two fronts, the German army could summon astonishing self-sacrificial reserves of fighting skill and spirit. It was here that organizational efficiency and experience counted. The high command may have been diseased, but lower down the Germans were often superb. In

A knocked-out German Tiger tank lies amongst the rubble of bomb-damaged buildings

Panzer Grenadiers ride into action

Normandy they became masters of small-scale defence, of holding back large forces, of striking when the Allies no longer had the benefit of artillery. Despite their privations, units from the Eastern Front did not collapse under pressure, retaining an ability to fight sometimes even when they had lost 75 per cent of their men. The Hitler Youth, with an average age of just 18, fought with a tenacity inspired by fanaticism. When units were mangled, ordinary soldiers readily took to sudden reassembly with survivors from other units into ad hoc battle groups to continue the fight. One study of the opposing forces (Col. Trevor Dupuy, *A Genius for War*) concluded baldly: "On a man for man basis, the German ground soldier consistently inflicted casualties at about a 50 percent higher rate than they incurred from the opposing British and American troops under all circumstances." If it had not been for Allied command of the skies, there would have been many more battles, and many opposite conclusions.

By contrast, British forces sometimes proved to be lacking in commitment, tactical skill and quality of leadership. Sluggishness, lack of flexibility and initiative, despondency, lack of determination, a failure of understanding between tanks and infantry: all these lacks were imputed then and since to various Allied units in the long battle for Normandy. Officers too often relied on set-piece infantry attacks. Fiercely proud regiments often refused co-operation with rival regiments. Men used to desert warfare were nonplussed by the claustrophobic bocage. In many, the strain of conflict proved intolerable. One battalion commander reported shell-shock, hysteria, self-inflicted wounds and a complete collapse of group identity: "It is no longer a battalion, but a collection of individuals. There is naturally no esprit de corps for those who are frightened (as we all are to one degree or another) to fall back on. I have twice had to draw my revolver on retreating men."

The American forces, too, suffered serious operational difficulties. Lack of communication between tanks and infantry often meant that infantry was left exposed. The infantry themselves often lacked the battle-hardness of their opponents. Yet these soldiers bore the brunt of the action: forming only 6 percent of the army, they took over half the casualties. In Normandy, where small groups were constantly having to fight away from larger units, low-level

Allied Battles Casualties 6–30 June 1944		
Status	U.S.	U.K. & Ca.
Killed	5,113	3,356
Wounded	26,538	15,815
Missing	5,383	5,527
TOTAL	**37,034**	**24,698**
Replaced	41,000	38,000

German Battles Casualties 6 June – 7 July 1944	
Status	Total killed, wounded, missing and POWs
Officers	1,830
Other Ranks	75,166
Russians	3,787
TOTAL	**80,783**

leadership was vital, and again was often lacking. "The average infantry soldier," ran one report, "places too much reliance upon the supporting artillery to drive the enemy from positions opposing his advance."

The causes of the differences between Allied and German fighting abilities have been much discussed. Perhaps, in the end, the explanation lies in the difference in motivation.

Many Allied soldiers felt that a great threat had been lifted. Once safely across the Channel they were victors, in all but name. But there was no new empire to be won, no great gain in restoring the status quo - merely a job to be done. The widespread belief that the war would soon be over often discouraged the taking of risks which could be avoided.

The Germans, on the other hand, had nothing to lose by fighting. They knew that the Allies' aim, as expressed by Roosevelt, was unconditional surrender. They were therefore facing the end not just of Nazism, not just of

an empire, but of their country, their self-respect, their very identity. As soldiers they obeyed and fought on to a degree that astonished the Allies. For those who did not surrender, there was nothing left to do but fight.

By July 1, after the collapse of Epsom, Montgomery also faced another severe constraint. There was a limit to the reinforcements he could call upon. Casualties had climbed to 25,000. Now, for every two casualties, there would only be one replacement. Though there were some 100,000 infantry in Britain, they were not committed to Normandy, an anomaly of British military planning that has never been explained. At any rate, in July 1944, Allied superiority - 25 divisions v. 18, which in fighting terms amounted to the equivalent of 14 - was no true indication of the dilemma Montgomery faced. The specter of stalemate still loomed. It was going to be a long and hard struggle.

A smoke-screen is laid and troops of the 6th Royal Scots Fusiliers make their way across a field to engage the enemy

6 BREAKTHROUGH, BREAK-OUT

On June 29 in Berchtesgaden, Rommel, backed by Rundstedt, again urged a rearguard action, falling back to the Seine. The British, he pointed out, had been stopped only by using all the reserves. If Hitler did not agree, the 7th Army would be destroyed and the 15th Army, still in the Pas de Calais, would not be able to withstand the expected second invasion.

Hitler would not hear of it. Ignoring realities, he made extravagant promises of winning a war of attrition. The two generals returned to France angry and disappointed. When a counterattack on the Odon failed two days later, von Rundstedt warned Keitel at OKW that this could be the beginning of the end.

"What shall we do?" wailed Keitel.

"Make peace, you fools," said Rundstedt. "What else can you do?"

The remark was passed to Hitler, who promptly fired Rundstedt, replacing him with Field-Marshal Günther Hans von Kluge. He had commanded the 4th Army's advances across France and Russia and then the hard-fought retreat

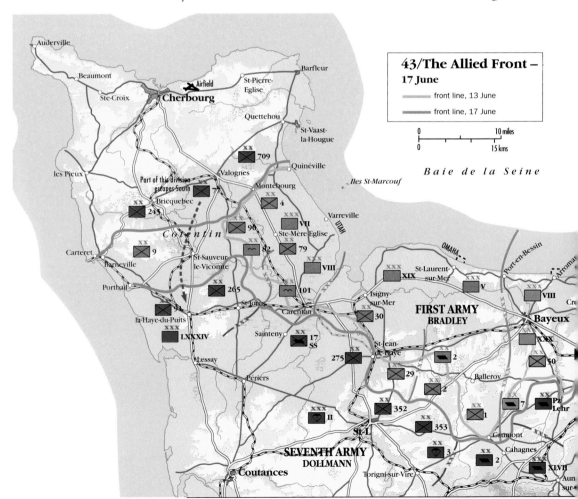

**43/The Allied Front –
17 June**

front line, 13 June
front line, 17 June

0   10 miles
0   15 kms

Baie de la Seine

from Russia as C-in-C of Army Group Center. Hitler liked him because he never questioned his Führer's orders. In fact, his loyalty was not absolute: he had considered joining the opposition to Hitler, only to pull back from direct involvement. It was von Kluge who had to face coming attempts by the Allies to enlarge their bridgehead.

With Cherbourg safely in Allied hands, the Americans now had a huge advantage in numbers in the Cotentin Peninsula – 14 divisions against the German's six – but they were constrained by geography. On the left lay the deep valley of the Vire and the Germans' strongpoint of St-Lô; in the center, the swamps of the flooded Taute, flanked by the only good road south, a bottleneck blocked by mines and felled trees; on the right, steep, wooded and well-defended hills. The whole area was a web from which Bradley longed to be free. "I didn't want to stand up and slug," he said, "but …while in this bocage, canalized by swamps we could do nothing else." These constraints, combined with stubborn resistance, blocked the assault on July 10, with only a few miles of land to show for the effort.

At the other end of the line, the British and Canadians renewed the assault on Caen. To advance, they would need to control the airfield at Carpiquet, the city's bridges over the Orne, and the roads leading eastwards. First, the Canadians assaulted Carpiquet, but found the airfield too firmly held to take.

A Cromwell tank on the way to the front passes through Hérouvillette

The attack on the city itself opened on the evening of July 7, when some 450 bombers dropped 2,500 tons of bombs on the northern outskirts of Caen, blasting even more of the ancient houses into rubble. But when the British and Canadians finally fought their way into the town street-by-street and house-by-house, they found every bridge across the Orne blown, and the Germans firmly facing them on the far bank.

Once again, stalemate seemed imminent. Four newly-arrived German infantry divisions had begun replacing the tanks around Caen, releasing them to harden the front against the Americans. Only a quick further advance would prevent German reinforcements drawing a line round the whole bridgehead. But Caen was deadlocked, and the Americans could do nothing to help just yet: Bradley told Montgomery his troops would have to resupply and capture St-Lô – the key to the main road that would take the Americans west – before there could be a significant advance, and that would take ten days.

At this dark time on July 11, Bradley hatched the idea that would finally break the log-jam. The plan – an operation codenamed Cobra – called for a U.S. advance south and then westwards to seize the rest of Brittany. Ports there would be vital to the continued build-up of Allied forces. Cobra might even become a "breakthrough" – a term that began to acquire a peculiar significance – a limited breakthrough, perhaps, but at least an escape from the bocage into more open country.

The delay left Montgomery with a problem: how to keep German armor concentrated on

Caen. He was helped by the fact that the Germans had reasons of their own for concentrating on Caen. For one thing, they still thought they had to reckon with a second landing in the Pas de Calais. For another, they were not committed simply to "drawing a line round the whole bridgehead." They were, by training, committed to attack. It was at Caen they had focused their diminishing hopes of counterattacking and driving the Allies into the sea.

It was Montgomery's Second Army commander, Miles Dempsey, who devised the strategy intended to drive back the Germans around Caen. It was a strategy designed to capitalize on the huge, and growing, reserves of armor, now amounting to some 2,250 medium and 400 light tanks. He had been impressed by the effects of the previous bombing attack on Caen, and determined to gain all the benefits he could from an aerial bombardment. Montgomery agreed.

The attack, set to begin on July 18, would be a tightly focused punch by some 750 tanks to the east of Caen, from the base established by the 6th Airborne, over the Orne, across cornfields, over two railway lines and up towards a well-defended ridge at Bourguébus, seven miles from the start line. This would be preceded by a feint on the other side of Caen across the Odon, and, only two hours before the assault proper, by a devastating aerial and naval bombardment to shatter the village strongholds dotted across the

U.S. Infantry probing the road into St-Lô. This infantryman carries a M1A1 rocket launcher, "Bazooka" anti-tank weapon as well as his Garand rifle

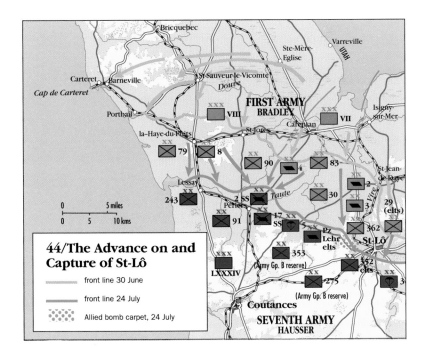

44/The Advance on and Capture of St-Lô

- front line 30 June
- front line 24 July
- Allied bomb carpet, 24 July

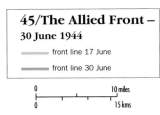

45/The Allied Front –
30 June 1944

- front line 17 June
- front line 30 June

0 _____ 10 miles

0 _____ 15 kms

Baie de la Seine

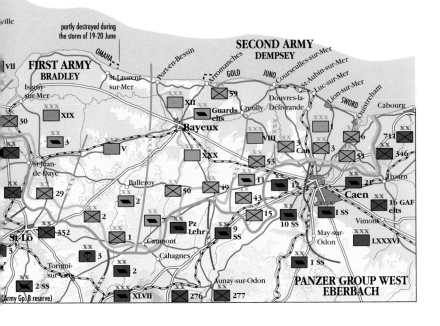

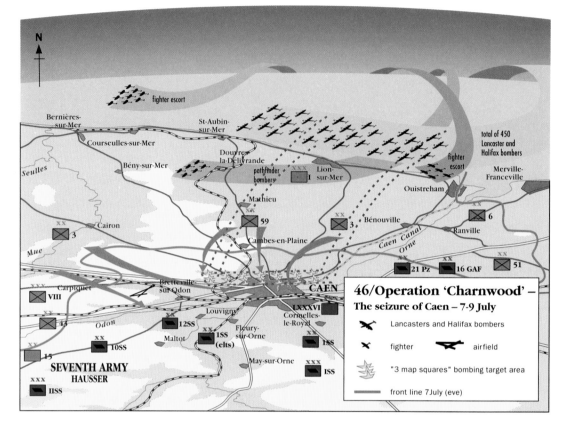

46/Operation 'Charnwood' –
The seizure of Caen – 7-9 July

✈ Lancasters and Halifax bombers

✖ fighter   ✈ airfield

"3 map squares" bombing target area

front line 7 July (eve)

gently rolling countryside. The bomber offensive would be the largest ever made in support of ground troops. The whole operation – codenamed Goodwood – would be followed in short order by Cobra, the "breakthrough" by the Americans at the other end of the line.

That was the intention, and it had the enthusiastic backing of both Bomber Command and SHAEF. Unfortunately, their enthusiasm was inspired in part by Dempsey's mention of Falaise as an eventual target, and in part by Montgomery's overweening optimism. Falaise lay over 20 miles to the south east. Although Monty revised the operation's aim at the last minute, saying that he hoped only to use armored cars to spread panic in the direction of Falaise, the revision was not passed to SHAEF where the top brass continued to believe that the attack would be one prong of a two-pronged break-through, and that Montgomery, in pursuit of his original conception, intended to drive on towards Paris. This was a misunderstanding that would spell trouble later.

No one doubted it would be a hard fight. No one knew how hard, though. Firstly, the whole area was much more heavily defended than the Allies realized. Rommel believed that by holding Caen he would prevent the illusory "second landing" in the Pas de Calais. For entirely the wrong reason, he and Panzer Group West's commander, General Heinrich Eberbach, had created a superb defence in five levels: infantry, panzers, a dozen fortified villages, the artillery (including almost 300 guns and another 272 six-barrelled Nebelwerfer mortars) on Bourguébus Ridge, and a further line of fortified villages, plus 45 Panthers and 80 medium tanks in reserve five miles further back.

Secondly, the Germans, from their base in the eastern suburbs of Caen, where the towers of a steelworks provided wonderful viewpoints, would see any attempt to bring up vehicles by daylight. To prevent this, the plan dictated that the three armored divisions move at night, and that only one actually cross the Orne. The other two – with over 8,000 vehicles between them – would wait until the action started; but there were only six crossing points. The logistics were a nightmare.

That problem was compounded by another. The British commanders suddenly realized that their own troops had laid a minefield right across the line of advance, and had done so hastily, without mapping the work closely. To preserve secrecy, the mines were to be lifted only at night. Since the field itself was now overgrown, uncharted and churned up by German shells, the task was impossible. All that could be done in the time was to clear 17 narrow corridors. The tanks would be constrained and slowed just when they need space and speed.

It was of no help at all to the Allies that when the time came for action, Rommel was out of it. On the afternoon of July 17, he was returning from the HQ of Panzer Group West to his own base in Roche-Guyon when his open-topped car was attacked by two Spitfires. Rommel ordered his driver to race for cover. As the car accelerated, it was caught by a burst of fire. The driver was hit, the car swerved into a tree, Rommel was thrown out, and sustained severe head injuries. His escorts carried him still unconscious into the nearest

Private Sutcliffe of Stockport, Cheshire, watches for enemy movements from his position in the suburbs of Caen

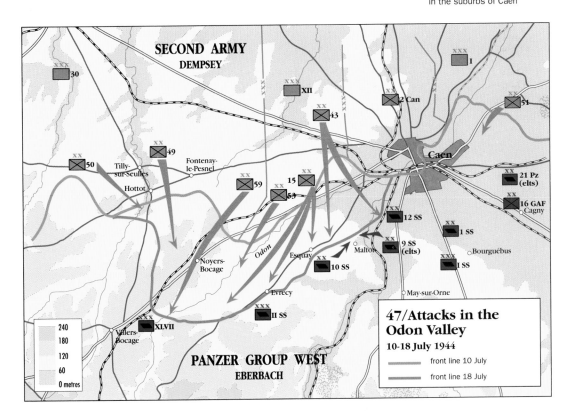

SECOND ARMY
DEMPSEY

30
XII
43
49
50
Tilly-sur-Seulles
Fontenay-le-Pesnel
Hottot
59
15
53
Noyers-Bocage
Odon
Esquay
Evrecy
10 SS
II SS
XLVII
Villers-Bocage

PANZER GROUP WEST
EBERBACH

Caen
I
2 Can
51
21 Pz (elts)
16 GAF
Cagny
12 SS
1 SS
9 SS (elts)
Malton
Bourguébus
I SS
May-sur-Orne

240
180
120
60
0 metres

47/Attacks in the Odon Valley
10-18 July 1944

——— front line 10 July
——— front line 18 July

Following an artillery barrage
British Infantry cautiously
advance through the ruins of
Tilly searching for German
snipers

village. He was never again fit enough for action, and was invalided home, leaving von Kluge to take over Army Group B, in effect running the whole Normandy campaign.

At dawn on July 18, a heavy aerial bombardment – the first of many that day from some 4,500 Allied aircraft – battered swathes of countryside up to Bourguébus Ridge for three hours. Ground and naval artillery fired 250,000 rounds, helping to create a maelstrom of earth, dust and smoke in which even the Tigers were buried or flipped over. It seemed that nothing could survive such treatment. Into this cratered and smoking graveyard the tanks and infantry of 11th Armoured Division began to advance, forming columns to cross the river and funnel through the minefield. For four miles the leading units advanced steadily.

Again, exhilaration turned to disappointment. As the leading units were tackling the embankment of the second railway line, five 88s and a Tiger opened up from the ruins of Cagny, another example of the way in which troops can survive apparently overwhelming bombardment to emerge fighting strongly and well, to the astonishment of their enemies. In Cagny, Colonel Hans von Luck, newly arrived from a short rest in Paris, found four of the 88s manned by Luftwaffe troops pointing their weapons skywards. Von Luck ordered them to fire on the oncoming tanks. They refused, at which von Luck drew his pistol and gave the Luftwaffe officer in charge a choice: co-operate or die. He co-operated, and in minutes the 88s had knocked out 16 British tanks.

Then, as other British units slipped past, infantry and anti-tank guns opened fire from other bombed and ruined villages, and finally from the ridge itself, where German tanks had a firm hold and well protected by buildings and sunken lanes.

Back near the Orne, the rest of the armor was still jockeying into lines to negotiate the minefield, funelling in and out of corridors in a massive traffic jam that gave no room for maneuver. Goodwood stalled, in the biggest tank battle of the campaign with the huge Tigers and Panthers holding off the more numerous, but more vulnerable Shermans and Cromwells. By evening Cagny had fallen, but the ridge was still held by the Germans' anti-tank guns.

For the next two days in a score of local actions, Allied forces took village after village, forcing the German front back and away from Caen, until a thunderstorm on the afternoon of July 20 put an end to Goodwood. The operation had gained at most seven miles, at a cost of some 6,000 casualties and almost 400 tanks. And no breakthrough.

The initial success, however, had inspired Montgomery to new heights of optimism – "operations this morning a complete success," he cabled to Eisenhower, and then that evening gave a press conference mentioning the loaded word "breakthrough." When the truth emerged, Eisenhower and the British Chiefs of Staff were horrified, both at the tenacity of the German defence and at what they judged to be Montgomery's failure. Eisenhower raged that "it had taken 7,000 tons of bombs to gain seven miles and that the Allies could hardly hope to go through France paying a price of 1,000 tons of bombs per mile." One commander, Air Chief Marshal Sir Arthur Tedder, suggested that Ike should sack Monty. Montgomery, of course, insisted that no breakthrough was intended, that progress was quite satisfactory since the British forces – or rather "I" as Monty called them – were now past three major obstacles: Caen, the Odon and the Orne. The controversy was, and remained, intense, not so much because of the plan and its execution but because of the clash of personality, expectation and reality. Huge issues were personified in apparently petty rows over Montgomery – his prima donna posturing and schoolboy insensitivity on the one hand, his military genius

A Sherman tank advances
through the center of Caen

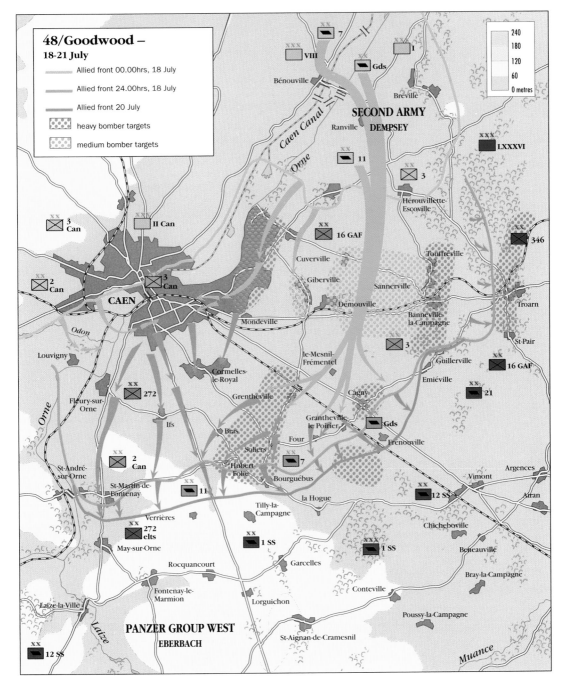

48/Goodwood –
18-21 July

Allied front 00.00hrs, 18 July

Allied front 24.00hrs, 18 July

Allied front 20 July

heavy bomber targets

medium bomber targets

240
180
120
60
0 metres

XX 7

XXX VIII

XX Gds

Bénouville

Caen Canal

Orne

SECOND ARMY
DEMPSEY

Ranville

Breville

XXX LXXXVI

XX 11

XX 3

Hérouvillette-
Escoville

XX 3
Can

II Can

XX 16 GAF

Touffréville

XX 346

Cuverville

Giberville

Sannerville

XX 2
Can

3
Can

Démouville

Banneville-
la-Campagne

Troarn

CAEN

Mondeville

St-Pair

Odon

le-Mesnil-
Frémentel

XX 3

Guillerville

Louvigny

Cormelles-
le-Royal

Emiéville

XX 16 GAF

XX 272

Grentheville

Cagny

XX 21

Fleury-sur-
Orne

Ifs

Grantheville-
le-Poirier

XX Gds

Bras

Four

Frenouville

Orne

Soliers

XX 2
Can

Hubert-
Folie

XX 7

Argences

St-André-
sur-Orne

Bourguébus

Vimont

Airan

St-Martin-de-
Fontenay

XX 11

la Hogue

XX 12 SS

Tilly-la-
Campagne

Chicheboville

Verrières

XX 272
elts

XX 1 SS

XXX 1 SS

Beneauville

May-sur-Orne

Rocquancourt

Garcelles

Bray-la-Campagne

Fontenay-le-
Marmion

Lorguichon

Conteville

Poussy-la-Campagne

Laize-la-Ville

Laize

PANZER GROUP WEST
EBERBACH

St-Aignan-de-Cramesnil

Muance

XX 12 SS

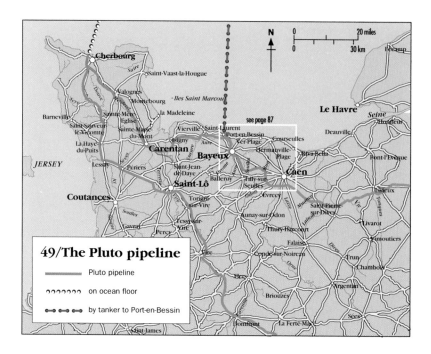

see page 87

49/The Pluto pipeline

— Pluto pipeline

ᴖᴖᴖᴖᴖᴖ on ocean floor

•-◦ •-◦ •-◦ by tanker to Port-en-Bessin

and inspirational leadership on the other. Field Marshal Sir Alan Brooke wrote in his diary that he was "tired to death with humanity and all its pettiness. Will we ever learn to 'love our Allies as ourselves'?"

However, Goodwood was not an out and out disaster. In part Monty was right, but in ways he could not have known at the time. Two Panzer divisions that were due to go to St-Lô to oppose the Americans were diverted to hold the line south of Caen. And the German High Command had been horrified to see their broad defensive system shattered by carpet bombing. The German right flank was a shadow of its former self. Von Kluge, appointed for his supposedly slavish determination to hold out, told Hitler "that in the face of the enemy's complete command of the air, there is no possibility of our finding a strategy that will counter-balance its truly annihilating effect, unless we give up the field of battle."

The threat, now seen clearly by all Germany's military leaders, inspired drama of an entirely different sort: the last and most famous attempt to kill Hitler.

There had been opposition to Hitler since before the war, mostly from within the armed forces. Several senior figures – notably von Kluge and Rommel – had been approached by the conspirators, and offered their tentative support, not to kill Hitler, but in the event of his being killed by others. Galvanized by defeat at Stalingrad in early 1943, the conspiracy had been undermined by the Allied insistence on total surrender, which, if Hitler was killed, would deprive his generals of any hope of remaining in power. Now, however, with defeat a near-certainty, the opposition had little left to lose. With Hitler dead, the conspirators could hope to offer terms that would carry some weight with the Allies, and thus preserve something of Germany. But once the Allies broke out of their bridgehead, Germany would be left with nothing with which to compromise. It was now or never. Everything was in place for the assassination. With the news of Hitler's death transmitted by his signals officer, the only member of his personal staff who was in the conspiracy, the Army would arrest leading Nazis, seize power, establish a new civil government and sue for peace.

The leading conspirator, Colonel Count Claus von Stauffenberg, had recently been appointed Chief of Staff to the Commander-in-Chief of the Home Army, Erich Fromm, whose deputy, Friedrich Olbricht, was also in the plot. Though Stauffenberg was hardly an ideal assassin, having lost an arm, two fingers of his remaining hand and an eye in the Tunisian campaign, he had good access to Hitler, and took on the role of executioner. Since he would also be co-ordinator of the post-coup government, it was vital that he survive the killing. Stauffenberg's chosen method of assassination was a bomb built into his briefcase, which he took with him to several meetings in July, never finding the right circumstances.

Another opportunity would come on July 20, in Hitler's HQ in Rastenburg, East Prussia (now in Poland), the so-called Wolfsschanze ("Wolf's Lair"), where Nazi leaders were to meet in Hitler's bomb-proof concrete bunker, an ideal structure that would contain the blast ensuring the deaths of all present.

Again, Stauffenberg was unlucky. The bunker was being reinforced so the meeting with Hitler and 23 others was to be held in a wooden shed used as a map room nearby. It was a hot day and the windows were open. Stauffenberg waited in his car until the conference was under way. Then he opened his case, pulled out the fuse-pin with his teeth, shut the case and walked in to join the conference. Placing the case under the huge map table just by Hitler, he murmured an excuse about needing to telephone, and left again. When he was 60 yards away the bomb exploded. Stauffenberg saw the pall of dust, smoke and debris, ran for his car and headed for Berlin.

The Signals Officer in Rastenburg released the news as planned. Quickly, in half a dozen cities, the army of conspirators took action, arresting Gestapo and SS officers. Stauffenberg arrived in Berlin and arrested his commander, Fromm. In France one of the conspirators, Colonel-General Karl von Stülpnagel, Military Governor in France, set out from Paris to convince von Kluge to sue for peace. But back in Berlin at the Propaganda Ministry, Goebbels had called Rastenburg and discovered that Hitler was alive. At 6.45, Berlin Radio carried the news. Not long afterwards, Von Kluge saw the transcript. "The bloody thing's misfired," he said acidly to Stülpnagel, and did nothing.

Hitler's survival was an astonishing piece of luck, for four others died in the blast. An officer had kicked the briefcase, and then moved it a few feet out of the way. When the explosion came, Hitler had been protected by the heavy table, and by the flimsiness of the hut, which had allowed the force of the blast to be dissipated. He had staggered from the smoking ruin, his right arm limp, but otherwise unhurt. Having ordered a clamp-down in communications, he was in a new uniform within half an hour and driving off to meet Mussolini who was arriving on an official visit to inspect some Italian troops. Only on his return, when he spoke to Goebbels, did he order action to suppress the conspiracy.

From that moment the conspirators, all of whom had revealed themselves, were as good as dead. Fromm had Stauffenberg and several others shot that evening. Over the coming months some 5,000 were executed and another 10,000 sent to concentration camps. Several committed suicide. One of those implicated was Rommel's Chief-of-Staff, Lt-General Hans Speidel. From Speidel it was a short step to Rommel himself, still recuperating in Ulm. Through two officers, Hitler offered him a choice: a public trial or suicide. He chose the latter. In an extraordinary display of hypocrisy, Hitler gave Rommel a State funeral and announced that he had died of wounds. In the days, weeks and months after the plot misfired, the Army was humiliated, all opposition crushed, and Hitler again supreme.

He was not, therefore, in any mood to accept von Kluge's opinion that the

Hitler shows Mussolini the devastation caused by the Stauffenberg bomb plot

General Jodl, Chief of the Wehrmacht Operations Staff

end was near. He simply ordered all his forces to stand fast, ignoring the lack of any means of making this possible.

In the previous three months, some 5,500 Luftwaffe fighters had been lost – 1,000 more than had been produced. Some 800 fighters transferred to France, hampered by bombed-out airfields and crushing Allied air attacks, were almost useless. Bombing raids into the Reich more than halved production of aviation fuel. Allied planes could bomb Normandy almost at will, precluding movement by day, cutting railways again and again, allowing road convoys just a few hours of darkness to ferry forward their scanty supplies of fuel and ammunition. By a miracle of organization, tank production remained high, but tanks could not be moved from their German factories to the front.

Meanwhile, the Allied build-up continued unchecked with some 54,000 tons of supplies landing daily over the remaining Mulberry, directly over the Omaha and Utah beaches, and, from mid-July, through Cherbourg. By July 20, seven weeks after the invasion, the Allies had landed 36 divisions: almost 1,500,000 men, with a ton of supplies per man and some 300,000 vehicles. If a breakthrough was vital for military reasons, it was equally so for logistical reasons. The bridgehead was full to bursting.

By July 20, as Hitler began to wreak terrible vengeance on his would-be killers and as Goodwood staggered to a halt the other side of Caen, the Americans were ready. St-Lô had fallen two days before. The German line, a mere nine divisions, was worn to breaking point by the battle for the Cotentin and by the need to keep armor, mortars and men to block the British around Caen. Bradley, by comparison, now had 15 divisions with his reserves building all the time.

He was ready to open Operation Cobra, to attempt a breakthrough with a sharp, restricted jab. For Bradley the idea of concentrating power – intensive carpet-bombing followed by a ground assault on a narrow front – was an original concept dictated by the unexpectedly restrictive nature of the bocage. It meant using heavy bombers and fighter-bombers (to minimize the massive craters left by heavies) closer to troops than ever before. Bradley believed he could rely on the bombers' accuracy if they used the main road west as a guide. The ground assault would then take American armor to that road, and along it westwards to the coast.

The Germans' only hope was that the American advance would be slowed by a hard-fought defence along the lanes of the labyrinthine bocage. It was a vain hope. Bradley had introduced intensive retraining to improve co-ordination between tanks, infantry and fighter-bombers. And the Americans now had the services of their own "funny," a newly-devised hedge-cutting tank known as a Rhinoceros with a formidable toothed prow that could remove a bocage bank – earth, roots, hedge and all – with hardly a pause.

A British patrol enters St. Mauviel still occupied by German troops

Caen, which fell to British and Canadian troops on 9 July, was heavily bombed by the Allies and further damaged in the fierce battle which led to its capture. Here a British soldier carries a little girl through a ruined street

The Americans would have the advantage of numbers, speed, mobility and efficiency.

Some of this advantage was lost by bad luck and bad judgement. The weather closed in again - the same storm that brought Goodwood to a halt - delaying the start of Cobra for four days. "Dammit," muttered Bradley, staring up at the leaden skies, "I'm going to have to court martial the chaplain if we have much more weather like this." Then, when the go-ahead finally came, continuing rain forced Bradley to cancel - not soon enough though to call back some 350 of the bombers. These were supposed to come in from the west, parallel to the American front, using a road leading to Périers as their base line. Instead they came in from the north over the heads of the troops. Lacking a clear view of their target, some dropped their bombs "short," on their own lines, killing 25 men. This disaster gave away the point of attack and might have had even more disastrous consequences - Bradley briefly wondered if he had a complete failure on his hands - if von Kluge had not still been sure that the main thrust would come at Caen. As it was, von Kluge kept his major force of panzers there.

An American machine gunner takes advantage of hedgerow cover during the Battle of St-Lô on 15 July 1944

Auderville

Beaumont

Ste-Croix

Cherbourg ✈ Airfield

St-Pierre-Eglise

Barfleur

Quettehou

St-Vaast-la-Hougue

les Pieux

Valognes

Quinéville

Montebourg

Varreville

Bricquebec

C o t e n t i n

XXX XV

Ste-Mère-Eglise

UTAH

Carteret

Barneville

St-Sauveur-le-Vicomte

FIRST ARMY
BRADLEY

XX 6

Portbail

Isigny-sur-Mer

Carentan

X

la-Haye-du-Puits

St-Jores

Sainteny

XXX VIII

XX 79

XX 8

XX 90

XX 4

XXX

XXX VII

St-Jean-de-Daye

XXX XI

XX 243

XX 355

Lessay

XX 83

XX 1

2

XXX

XX 17 SS

3

XX 9

XX 5

XX 30

XX 35

XXX LXXXIV

Pz Lehr part

XX 29

St-Lô

XX

XX 352

SEVENTH ARMY
HAUSSER

Coutances

XXX II

Torigni-sur-

0 ————— 10 miles
0 ————— 15 km

50/The Allied Front –
24 July 1944

front line 30 June
front line 24 July

When Cobra finally started on July 25, it still came as a shock to the Germans. Fighter-bombers raked outposts, 1,500 Fortresses and Liberators carpet-bombed a front four miles wide, and then, as the infantry advanced, medium bombers battered the main road west from St-Lô. Again the bombers failed to follow directions, and again American bombs rained down on American troops, wounding 490 and killing 111 (among them a Lieutenant-General, Lesley McNair, commander of Army Ground Forces, the highest-ranking American to die in the campaign). Air Force commanders never took any blame for this tragedy, concluding in an investigation that the bombing was "within the normal expectancy of errors."

This shocking, demoralizing disaster slowed the advance, but against such a devastating assault the Germans could do little. "By noon nothing was visible but dust and smoke," Panzer Lehr's commander, Lt-Gen. Fritz Bayerlein, said in a post-war interview, "My front line looked like a lunar landscape and at least 70 percent of my troops were out of action – dead, wounded, crazed or numbed." It was astonishing that Panzer Lehr could put up any resistance at all, but they did, for two days, until Lightnin' Joe Collins's tanks broke through the crumbling facade. After that there was nothing left but retreat.

On the 27th American tanks, half-tracks and artillery rumbled south and west, using roads where they could but with Rhinos punching routes

A German soldier nervously carries a white flag of surrender towards the Americans during the battle of St-Lô

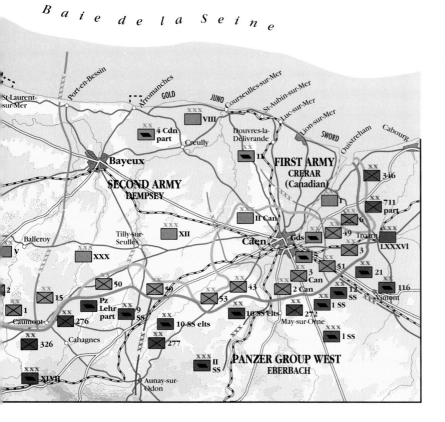

through hedgerows around mines and strongpoints. Above ranged Thunderbolt fighter-bombers, rocketing German positions pinpointed by ground forces. By the end of the 28th, the Americans had advanced 15 miles, and had taken Coutances. Reinforcements seized by von Kluge from Caen were too slow, too late, and too shattered by aerial attacks to help.

At this point one of the campaign's best known generals, George Patton, came to the fore. Already notorious for his flamboyance – his bouts of anger, his pearl-handled pistols, a love of publicity that outdid Montgomery – "Old Blood and Guts" had a somewhat strained relationship with his commander, Bradley. The two had been together in Sicily, where Patton had been the boss, Bradley the subordinate. There, Bradley had had his fill of Patton's rages and profanity, and he had been disgusted by the two famous incidents in which Patton slapped two soldiers accused of malingering. His career survived, just, because he was too brilliant to ignore. Now he was in command of the Third Army, recently landed and not yet fully operational. Eisenhower gave him VIII Corps and told him to head south.

Patton drove the 4th Armored Division, VIII Corps' spearhead, hard; by the evening of July 30, the first Americans were beyond Avranches, into Brittany. In five days, Cobra had turned from stasis, even possible disaster, into the mobile war of which the Allied commanders had dreamed. At last, a real breakthrough was possible. Patton had before him the chance of a lifetime, and he was just the right person to seize it.

That breakthrough could only happen if opposition was kept to a minimum – if, in other words, the main German force could be kept tied down around Caen. To do that, Montgomery had to attack. Not, however, close to Caen itself. There, a Canadian assault coinciding with Cobra had been halted by a shield that Montgomery had no wish to tackle again. Instead, in an operation codenamed Bluecoat, Montgomery told Dempsey to seize high ground dominated by Mt Pinçon south of Caumont and Villers-Bocage. Here, the Germans were firmly dug in, defended by large minefields.

Despite the now-usual bombardment by 1,000 heavy bombers on the morning of July 30, the minefields stymied a rapid advance until nightfall, when an infantry battalion of 11th Armoured discovered an unguarded trail through woods leading to an intact bridge. Summoned by radio, six tanks made it across, leading a spearhead south towards Vire which lay a mile inside the boundary between British and American forces. Not only did the Allies now threaten a town guarding five crucial roads that gave access to all the surrounding country, but they had begun to outflank Mt Pinçon and had also driven a six-mile-wide wedge between the two German armies, the 5th Panzer (as Panzer Group West had been renamed) and the 7th.

A scene in the center of the devastated town of Coutances with elements of the American 91st Division advancing

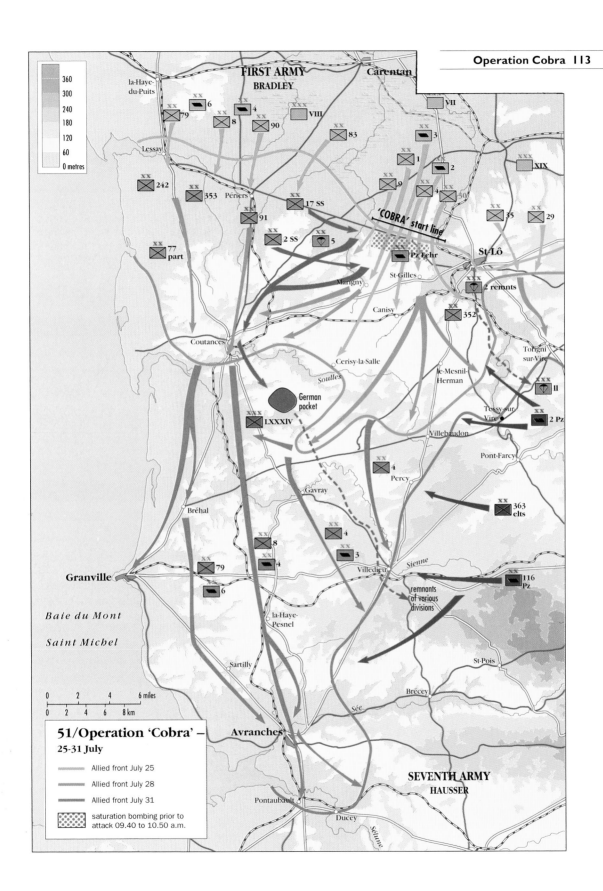

First Army
Bradley

la-Haye-
du-Puits

Carentan

VIII

VII

360
300
240
180
120
60
0 metres

79

6

8

4

90

83

3

XIX

1

2

Lessay

242

353

Périers

91

17 SS

9

4

35

29

'COBRA' start line

77
part

2 SS

5

Pz Lehr

St-Lô

Marigny

St-Gilles

2 remnts

Canisy

352

Coutances

Cerisy-la-Salle

Soulles

le-Mesnil-
Herman

Torigni-
sur-Vire

German
pocket

11

LXXXIV

Tessy-sur-
Vire

2 Pz

Villebaudon

Pont-Farcy

4

Percy

Gavray

363
elts

Bréhal

8

4

3

Villedieu

Sienne

116
Pz

Granville

79

4

remnants
of various
divisions

6

Baie du Mont

St-Pois

la-Haye-
Pesnel

Saint Michel

Sartilly

Brécey

0   2   4   6 miles
0   2   4   6   8 km

Sée

Avranches

SEVENTH ARMY
HAUSSER

51/Operation 'Cobra' –
25-31 July

Pontaubault

Ducey

Sélune

Allied front July 25

Allied front July 28

Allied front July 31

saturation bombing prior to
attack 09.40 to 10.50 a.m.

Montgomery and Bradley review plans. Meetings like this one in the bocage were crucial for measuring, and anticipating, the campaign's progress

The British ignored Vire, keeping to their objective - the seizure of Mt Pinçon - planning to leave Vire to the Americans. They pressed on eastwards only to be halted by some tough, clever little battlegroups - two or three tanks working with a few infantry and a mortar troop - formed from the remnants of Panzer reserves moving west. Further north, other objectives on the flanks of Mt Pinçon remained untaken, causing Dempsey to dismiss both Bucknall, 30th Corps commander, and Erskine, commander of the Desert Rats, and bringing Bluecoat to a halt on August 4.

Mt Pinçon still had to be taken by the British. The battle that followed on August 6 was one of the hardest in the whole campaign, not only for its fighting but also for the physical burden it imposed on the attackers. Mt Pinçon was only 1,200 feet high but its western slopes, where the British attacked, were steep and rough. The final assault opened around midday. It was hot and the air was thick with dust and the smell of dead cattle. An attack across a little river was stopped by heavy fire until tanks and infantry rushed a bridge leading to a village, la Varinière, from which half a dozen tanks managed to grind up a narrow track to the summit. From here they could dominate the area but they would need rapid reinforcement.

The task fell to the 4th Wiltshire Regiment waiting in reserve a mile to the north. The men were already exhausted for the previous day they had fought a savage battle for a village to the south, then that night force-marched seven miles behind the lines up to their present position, losing some 50 men to shellfire along the way. Now, as night fell, they had to climb 1,200 feet as fast as possible, carrying weapons, ammunition, picks and shovels. It took them all night. When they found the tanks, they were so exhausted that many men fell asleep as they dug themselves in, "falling headlong pick in hand into the half-dug trenches," in the words of one of the company commanders. Thus ended a battle both against Germans and against "the burning sun, the choking dust, our parched throats and empty bellies, the craggy slopes and tangled thickets, the rocky earth and above all our utterly weary bodies."

Together, Bluecoat and the seizure of Mt Pinçon served a vital purpose: when the action ended, tanks of the 1st and 9th SS Panzer Divisions were moving west across the Orne, weakening the defence of Caen.

To the west the Americans had been pouring across Brittany since July 30. They were virtually unopposed - except for the coast, Brittany was largely in the hands of French guerrillas. The main danger spot was the bridge at Avranches which the Germans failed to breach despite repeated bombing attacks. Through that bottleneck Patton shovelled seven divisions in three days. The columns of vehicles simply filed away along interior roads - the 6th

Armored towards Brest, 4th Armored towards Rennes – as densely-packed as Parisians on holiday. There was little between them and the far end of the peninsula some 130 miles to the west.

Nor anything much in any other direction. Patton was ecstatic: without the need for a slow-and-steady reduction of Brittany, there was nothing to stop a scything advance through the thinly-held Orleans Gap to the Seine, undercutting the whole miserable stalemate between Caumont and Caen. First Bradley agreed, then Montgomery, and finally Eisenhower. At a stroke – Patton's stroke – Overlord had acquired a new strategy, new dynamism, new morale.

In three days, August 4–7, American forces simply ballooned outwards, sweeping down towards the Loire, 60 miles south, and eastwards towards Le Mans, forming a bulge of occupied territory. Here the roads were long and straight, the countryside open, the defences minimal. There was nothing to stop them forming the southern claw of a pincer, with the British and Canadians making the northern claw. Between them, and trapped by the Seine beyond, von Kluge's armies were quite clearly about to be pinioned. All would be lost if the surviving German forces did not retreat at once.

Hitler, of course, did not see it that way. On August 4, he ordered a counterattack between Vire and Mortain, eight miles to the south. His intention was to cut the American forces in two by slicing through to Avranches, recapturing the neck of the Cotentin Peninsula, and thus severing the American armies from their supplies. This, he said, would effect "a complete reversal."

He was right: it would. It was also an utter fantasy. The Seventh Army would have to throw in everything it had, seizing troops and tanks from elsewhere, and still the action would be suicidal. The front would be fatally weakened, and the attack would probably fail anyway, but von Kluge, to whom the order came as a "thunderbolt," knew Hitler well enough to accept the inevitable. If attack he must, then the sooner the better, before his position worsened yet again. He planned the assault for two days later. Given the pressure from the British to the north and the Americans to the south, he could muster only four divisions fielding 250 tanks – half the number Hitler had demanded.

When the German attack was due to start, at midnight on the 6th, leading units were still moving up and others lacked the promised tanks and guns. The assault opened with only 100 tanks, and against a well-prepared enemy – the Americans had received a few hours' warning from decoded German signals. The 2nd SS Panzer Division managed to strike forwards a few miles, but elsewhere the Germans made little progress. Next morning they were helped by fog but when that lifted British and American fighter-bombers, entirely unopposed by any of the 300 German fighters von Kluge had been promised, pulverized the columns. The whole attack ground to a halt.

When the Americans began their flanking moves, backed by further thrusts further south towards Le Mans, the end was near. Von Kluge, trapped by Hitler's orders, still could not concede. On August 8, he ordered a Panzer division, the 9th, to move from Le Mans to Mortain to make another attempt to break through where 2nd Panzer had stalled. Hausser, commander of the Seventh Army, rightly protested that this would "deal a death blow not only to Seventh Army but to the entire Wehrmacht in the West." Von Kluge of course knew this too. What neither knew was that the end was so near: it had already started. In any event, von Kluge was both helpless and frightened. The witch-hunt for those implicated in the July 20 plot was in full swing, and might only be a matter of time before he was implicated. He needed to demonstrate a blind loyalty far beyond anything he felt.

"It is the Führer's order," he said, and committed his forces to oblivion.

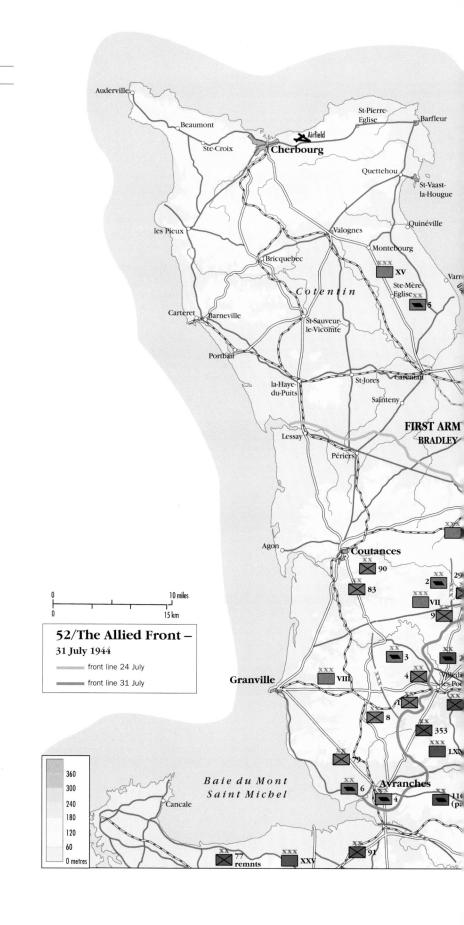

Auderville

Beaumont

St-Pierre-
Eglise

Barfleur

Airfield

Ste-Croix

Cherbourg

Quettehou

St-Vaast-
la-Hougue

les Pieux

Valognes

Quinéville

Montebourg

Bricquebec

XXX XV

C o t e n t i n

Ste-Mère-
Eglise XX

Varr

5

Carteret

Barneville

St-Sauveur-
le-Vicomte

Portbail

la-Haye-
du-Puits

St-Jores

Carentail

Saiñteny

FIRST ARM
BRADLEY

Lessay

Périers

Agon

Coutances

XXX

XX 90

XX 2   29

XX 83

XXX VII

XX 9

XXX 3

XX 4

XX
Villedi
les-Poe

XXX VIII

XX

Granville

52/The Allied Front –
31 July 1944

front line 24 July

front line 31 July

XX 8

XX 353

XXX LXX

XX 79

*Baie du Mont
Saint Michel*

XX 6

Avranches

XX 4

XX 11
(pa

Cancale

0   10 miles

0   15 km

360
300
240
180
120
60
0 metres

XX 77
remnts

XXX XXV

XX 91

7 FALAISE: "A SIGHT THAT PIERCED THE SOUL"

As the Germans defences weakened south of Caen, Montgomery's planned advance to Falaise and beyond became more than a possibility. Its execution would be in the hands of Lt-General Henry Crerar and his recently created 1st Canadian Army, a mixed bag that also included British, Polish, Czech, Belgian, Dutch and American units. Details of the assault – codenamed Totalize – were devised by the II Canadian Corps' commander, Lt-General Guy Simonds, notoriously sharp in both manner and intellect.

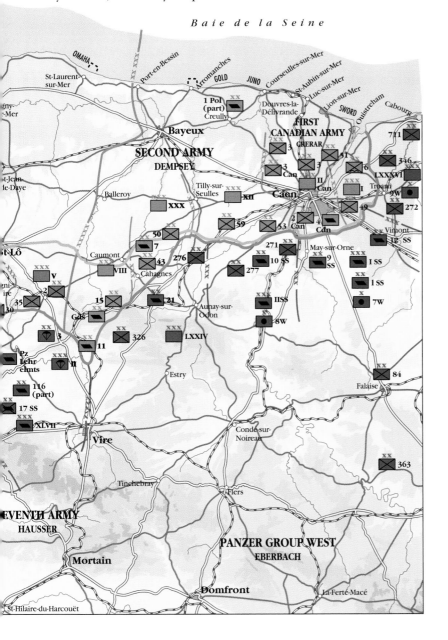

An M 10 loaded with Infantrymen passes through Caumont in pursuit of the retreating Germans. The offensive south of Caumont gained 10 miles in 24 hours on 2 August 1944

His problem, well defined by previous Allied actions, was that the four elements of attack – bombers, infantry, armor and artillery – normally struck in sequence, allowing the Germans to recover. He needed to co-ordinate forces to mount a simultaneous attack. The infantry could not simply march forward or be carried forward in vulnerable trucks. They had to be delivered on time, on target and in safety. His answer was brilliantly original. He planned to dispense with the standard pre-ground-attack aerial bombardment. Instead he would use armor to launch infantry into action. Part of the armored column would consist of a new type of vehicle devised by Simonds himself – self-propelled guns known as "Priests" with the 105mm guns removed, thus turning them into "defrocked Priests," as Simonds called them. These machines, carrying 11 infantrymen each, became better known as "Kangaroos," after the codename for the operation in which 250 men converted 76 Priests in three days. The armored columns would drive like spears through the flanks of the enemy defences. Moreover, to evade the deadly effects of machine-guns, mortars and 88s – Bourguébus Ridge was still strongly held by German artillery – the attack would come at night. Night-bombers patrolling the flanks of the attack would hold back German reinforcements. The next day heavy bombers would blast a way forward through the last of the defences. By the end of the day Allied forces would be out and on the way to Falaise.

Not only had no one ever tried anything like this before, it was also very risky. It demanded pinpoint accuracy by the night-bombers and by ground forces – if either went off course it would spell disaster for the troops. Radio beams, tracer-fire, shells that exploded with a green blast, and searchlights would all be used to mark a path in the darkness.

The four columns, four vehicles abreast, gathered either side of the main Caen–Falaise road on the evening of August 7 and 1,000 vehicles – tanks,

Sherman tanks moving forward for the attack on Mont Pinçon kick up clouds of dust on the road near Aunay-sur-Odon

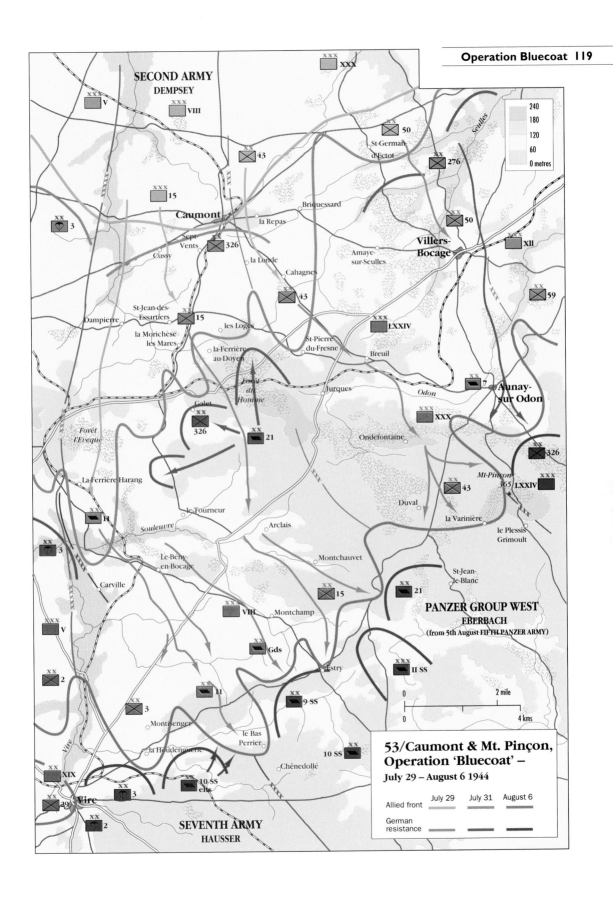

SECOND ARMY
DEMPSEY

XXX

XXX V

XXX VIII

XXX 50
St-German-
d'Ectot

XX 276

XX 43

XXX 15

Caumont   la Repas

Briquessard

XX 3

XX 50

XX XII

Sept.
Vents   XX 326

Cussy

la Londe

Amaye-
sur-Seulles

Villers-
Bocage

XX 59

Dampierre

St-Jean-des-
Essartiers   XX 15

la Morichèse
les Mares

Cahagnes

les Loges

XX 43

la Ferrière-
au-Doyen

St-Pierre-
du-Fresne

Breuil

XXX LXXIV

XX 7

Aunay-
sur Odon

Forêt
du
Homme

Jurques

Odon

XXX XXX

XX 326

Galet   XX 326

XX 21

Ondefontaine

XX 326

Forêt
l'Evêque

La-Ferrière-Harang

le-Tourneur

Mt-Pinçon
XX 43   365 LXXIV XXX

Duval

la Varinière

le Plessis
Grimoult

XX 11

Souleuvre

Arclais

XX 3

Le-Bény-
en-Bocage

Montchauvet

St-Jean-
le-Blanc

XX 21

PANZER GROUP WEST
EBERBACH
(from 5th August FIFTH PANZER ARMY)

Carville

XX 15

XXX V

XX VIII   Montchamp

XX 2

XX Gds

Estry

XXX II SS

XX 3

XX 11

0   2 mile

0   4 kms

Montisenger

le Bas
Perrier

XX 9-SS

10 SS   XX

53/Caumont & Mt. Pinçon,
Operation 'Bluecoat' –
July 29 – August 6 1944

la Houdenguerie

Chênedollé

XX XIX

XX 10 SS
elts

XX 3

Vire

XX 29

SEVENTH ARMY
HAUSSER

XX 2

	July 29	July 31	August 6
Allied front			
German resistance			

240
180
120
60
0 metres

Seulles

Vire

anti-tank artillery and Kangaroos – packed tight as rush-hour traffic. Just before midnight and flanked by a barrage, the vehicles rolled forward into what was soon an impenetrable swathe of dust and smoke lit in ghostly fashion by searchlights playing on the clouds – "Monty moonshine," as the men called it. For most of them there was nothing to be seen ahead but a pair of tail lights. The armor jostled forward slowly with many vehicles colliding or toppling into bomb-craters or wandering off into the darkness. "The chaos was indescribable," commented Lt-Col. A. Jolly. "The blind were leading the blind." Jolly, like other officers, restored order by blazing a trail with Very lights. Fortunately there was not far to go. By dawn on August 8 the Allies had cut three miles through the enemy lines. By evening the leading units formed the bow-wave of a bulge five miles deep.

This German tank has just been knocked out by bazooka fire. A detachment of Infantry led by 1st Sgt. James F. Kelly of Boston, Mass. run towards it to check for survivors from the crew

Thrown into utter confusion by such strange tactics, some of the fleeing Germans were stopped by the commander of the 12th SS Panzer Division, Kurt Meyer, who drove them back to their abandoned positions around the village of Cintheaux. Here they formed a core of German-held territory, holding up the inexperienced Canadians and Poles. It was during this advance that Michael Wittmann, hero of Villers-Bocage, died when his Tiger tank was smashed by five Shermans.

Simonds tried to break this deadlock with a night-time advance to a hill half way between Cintheaux and Falaise, only to have the column lose its way and then, at dawn, to run into a battery of 88s and Meyer's determined 12th SS Panzers which had 48 of their own tanks plus 19 Tigers from the 101st SS Heavy Tank Battalion. It took another day – August 9 – to take the hill and for the Germans to pull back to their next line of defence, the River Laison, protected by anti-tank guns in a wood near Quesnay and on a ridge at Potigny. The Germans were left with just 35 tanks with which to oppose the Canadians' 700, but still they held.

At this time a further advance might have been possible if Montgomery had ordered up reinforcements to harden the Canadians. They could have done with it for they were volunteers and were notoriously sluggish in their attacks. Historians have concluded that weight added to the Canadian thrust would have preserved momentum and shortened the grim engagements that followed. Bradley and his staff, muttering darkly about British overcaution, failed to understand why Montgomery did not supply reinforcements. It is a decision that has never been explained by Montgomery or anyone else.

Von Kluge had little respite. The first attack at Mortain on August 7 trapped 700 Americans of the 120th Infantry on a hill east of the town, reducing their fighting strength by almost 50 percent over the next five days, yet failed to

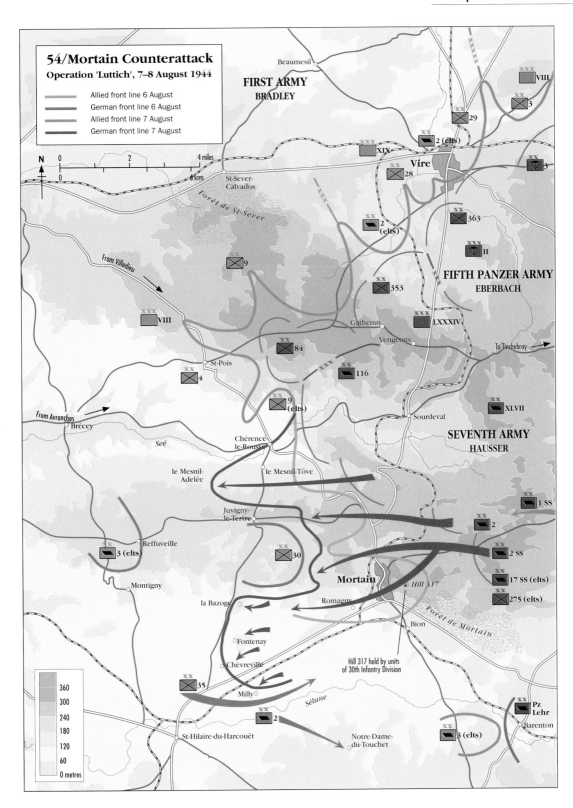

54/Mortain Counterattack
Operation 'Luttich', 7–8 August 1944

Allied front line 6 August
German front line 6 August
Allied front line 7 August
German front line 7 August

N

0   2   4 miles
0   8 kms

FIRST ARMY
BRADLEY

Beaumesil

VIII

3

29

2 (elts)

St-Sever-
Calvados

XIX

Vire

28

3

Forêt de St-Sever

2
(elts)

363

II

From Villedieu

9

FIFTH PANZER ARMY
EBERBACH

353

VIII

Gathemo

LXXXIV

To Tinchebray

84

Vengeons

St-Pois

116

4

Sourdeval

SEVENTH ARMY
HAUSSER

9
(elts)

XLVII

From Avranches

Brécey

Seé

Chérencé-
le-Roussel

le Mesnil-
Adelée

le Mesnil-Tôve

1 SS

Juvigny-
le-Tertre

2

3 (elts)

Reffuveille

2 SS

Montigny

30

17 SS (elts)

Mortain

Hill 317

275 (elts)

la Bazoge

Romagny

Bion

Forêt de Mortain

Fontenay

Chèvreville

Hill 317 held by units
of 30th Infantry Division

35

Milly

Sélune

Pz
Lehr

Barenton

St-Hilaire-du-Harcouët

2

Notre-Dame-
du-Touchet

3 (elts)

360
300
240
180
120
60
0 metres

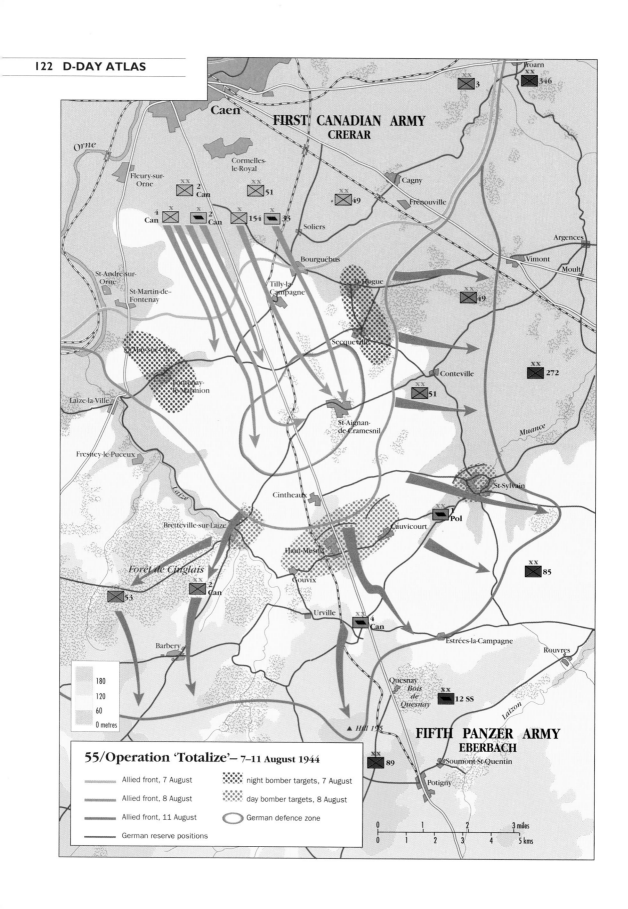

FIRST CANADIAN ARMY
CRERAR

FIFTH PANZER ARMY
EBERBACH

55/Operation 'Totalize'– 7–11 August 1944

Allied front, 7 August

Allied front, 8 August

Allied front, 11 August

German reserve positions

night bomber targets, 7 August

day bomber targets, 8 August

German defence zone

180
120
60
0 metres

Sherman tanks pass a
crashed Spitfire fighter as
they move up to Tilly-sur-
Seulles

take the hill or to punch a hole in Allied lines. Von Kluge could see clearly
the chance this gave the Allies. If the Americans came up from the south
toward Argentan, and if there was a further breakthrough in the north, von
Kluge's Seventh Army would be trapped. It was fearful dilemma. He could
only save his forces by withdrawing. There was a window of opportunity as
the American advance was slowed by Patton's determination to seize all of
Brittany. But time was running out and it would take a day at least to wring a
change of heart from Hitler. There was none. When von Kluge asked
permission to transfer a Panzer group away from Mortain to counter the
Canadians, Hitler suspected him of treachery. No permission came.

The Allies had already seen the tremendous chance they had been
granted. The agreed strategy through the first week of August was to drive to
the Seine, there bottling up the retreating Germans. Now an even more
dramatic possibility presented itself, as Bradley explained to Eisenhower on
August 8. He said American forces should be able to make a short, sharp "left
hook" up towards the Canadians and the British, trapping the Germans
around Falaise. As Bradley explained to the U.S. Secretary of the Treasury,
Henry Morgentau, then on a visit to the war zone, it was "an opportunity that
comes to a commander not more than once a century." He exaggerated –
Hitler's invasion of Russia and his defeat at Stalingrad involved far greater
gains and losses - but in the western European theater of war the prospect
was inspiring. "When the enemy loses his Seventh Army in this bag," Bradley
said, pointing at the bulge of German-held territory straddling the Orne, "he'll
have nothing left with which to oppose us. We'll be all the way from here to
the German border."

Montgomery agreed and a new tactic emerged. But the Americans could
not do both things at once - they could not make a short left hook and also
lunge for the Seine. Too many of them were tied up clearing the Mortain
bulge and Brittany. It had to be one then the other, in sequence - a sequence
that could be upset if anything went wrong, if for any reason the two pincers
did not close quickly enough to achieve what Bradley proposed.

On August 11 von Kluge could not escape the truth any longer. He was
trapped. In the south, Patton's Third Army was advancing on the vital supply
base of Alençon. In the north, the British and Canadians battered their way
forward another three miles. Careful to associate his opinion with those of
impeccable loyalty – SS General Hausser and the faithful Nazi Eberbach – von
Kluge told Hitler that the Mortain offensive was not possible now. Hitler at

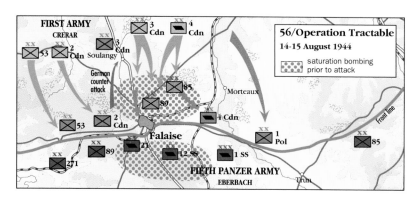

56/Operation Tractable
14-15 August 1944

saturation bombing prior to attack

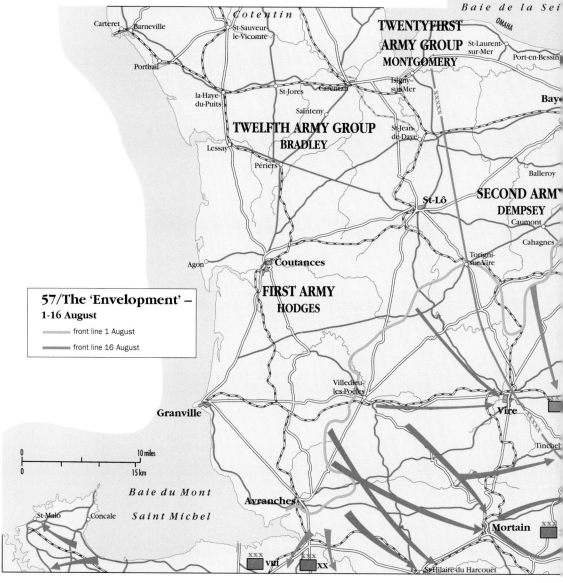

57/The 'Envelopment' –
1-16 August

front line 1 August
front line 16 August

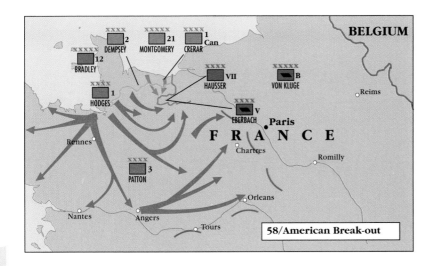

58/American Break-out

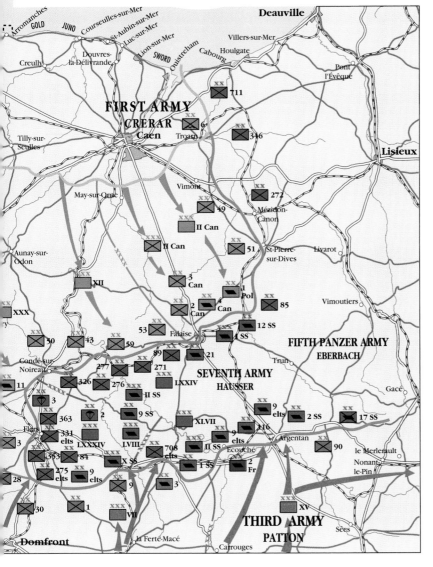

A Churchill tank makes its way across country near St.Pierre Torentaine

last gave his approval. The Seventh Army could withdraw, though Hitler's orders – totally ignoring the exhaustion of the Seventh Army, their lack of equipment and their daily crucifixion by Allied bombers and fighters – were to retain "the purpose of resuming the offensive westwards to the sea," and plan accordingly.

Every German general in the west now knew the end was near. Everywhere news was bad. In Italy the Allies were working their way northwards. In Russia Stalin's summer offensive had forced the Germans back beyond the 1939 frontier. In Normandy only the SS, still bound and blinded by loyalty, could deny the imminence of defeat. Yet, in the wake of the July 20 plot and its dreadful aftermath, no one dared tell Hitler the truth: that his forces were in tatters, his Army troops eager only to get home, his Army commanders frozen by impending catastrophe and terrorized by SS commanders who were convinced of the Army's treachery. When a number of senior officers urged the most respected of tank commanders, Sepp Dietrich, to approach Hitler, Dietrich replied: "If I want to get shot, that's the way to do it."

The whole idea of preparing for yet another attack was at once overtaken by events. Once again the Americans displayed their astonishing and headline-grabbing ability to move fast, much to the chagrin of the harder-pressed and exhausted British and Canadians. On the 12th the Americans took Alençon and swept on another 35 miles towards Argentan, 15 miles from Falaise and just 20 miles from the British and Canadians. Patton was delighted. "Push on slowly direction of Falaise," he ordered in cablese. "Upon arrival Falaise, continue to push on slowly until you contact our Allies."

It seemed the two arms of the pincers could snap shut in a day. After fending off some fierce resistance from Eberbach's Panzers, there didn't seem anything to stop Patton. "Shall we continue," he asked Bradley flippantly, "and drive the British into the sea for another Dunkirk?" Bradley overruled him, bringing his forces to a halt on the edge of Argentan on the boundary set by Montgomery between the two Allied forces.

This decision was – and remains – controversial. It countered his own strategy for trapping the Seventh Army with a push to Falaise. Later he blamed Montgomery for not moving faster to close the gap. True, Monty had not dreamed up the plan and he was later accused of a deliberate lack of drive. This was unfair. Difficult and prickly he might have been, but he was not the man to prejudice victory by sabotaging jointly-agreed plans. He was as keen as anyone to close the gap. On the 13th Crerar noted in his diary Monty's intention "to complete the firm juncture with the Third Army as soon as this can be arranged."

Why did Bradley himself not move? He felt it would invite a disaster, saying he "preferred a solid shoulder at Argentan to a broken neck at Falaise." Historians have had field days wondering why he feared a broken neck. He claimed that to cross the inter-forces boundary would have risked an exchange with the British and the other Allies advancing south – there had been little contact between the forces and it is always hard to recognize friend from foe in action. But this danger was well understood and well planned for. More likely, he suspected that Patton's three divisions would be overstretched, American lives would be needlessly sacrificed, and that Patton would need reinforcements that might weaken the advance eastwards due to start on August 15. "Normally, destruction of the enemy's army is the first objective of any force," he wrote in his memoirs. "Was a Seine River bridgehead important enough to warrant our rejecting that military tenet?" His answer, at that moment, was yes. "If Montgomery wants help in closing the gap, I thought, then let him ask for it. Since there was little likelihood of him asking, we would push on to the east." In brief, he opted for certain victory in the near future rather than a risky quick kill immediately.

Whatever the reasons, Monty's failure to reinforce and Bradley's decision to stop short would soon leave a gap between Argentan and Falaise that would offer a bolt-hole to the beleaguered Germans, fuel antagonism between Eisenhower and Monty, and spark a controversy that has rumbled on ever since.

As von Kluge told Jodl by teleprinter on the evening of the 13th the Fifth Panzer Army and Seventh Army were about to be encircled. Still he could not bring himself to suggest all-out retreat. Instead he proposed a pull-back to Flers, supposedly to release forces for the next attack. With the request phrased in this face-saving way, Hitler agreed.

Again events made a nonsense of such a limited response when the Canadians made their next move towards Falaise. The main obstacle was a screen of anti-tank guns defending Falaise in Quesnay Wood and Potigny Ridge. Simonds decided to bomb the guns into impotence and then by-pass them by crossing the Laison River and breaking through the German lines. As in Totalize, tanks would again lead the way for infantry carried in Kangaroos while bombers and artillery pounded the enemy lines from a distance. This time the advance would be under the cover of a smoke-screen, not darkness. Drivers would head for the sun showing through the smoke as a red disc.

When the attack came at noon on August 14, disaster struck the Canadians when bomber squadrons – including several Canadian squadrons – bombed short, causing 300 casualties. Despite this Simonds' novel tactics again succeeded in throwing the Germans into confusion. Battered by bombs and shells and blinded by smoke, the first they saw of the Allied armor was when it emerged through the clouds of smoke and dust. Again, in the strength and flexibility of their resistance, the Germans put up an astonishing performance, proving masters of the improvised battle group, the hard-fought engagement and the quick withdrawal. For two days 500 troops with 15 tanks and a dozen 88s held their ground on the last rise before Falaise. It fell on the 16th to Canadians moving in from the west, thus narrowing the gap with the American forces to 12 miles.

When the Canadians entered Falaise most of the Seventh Army were still west of the Orne. Only one unit – 2nd SS Panzer Corps – had been withdrawn by von Kluge, increasingly depressed by Hitler's intransigence and afraid he was about to be arrested for his nebulous connection with the July 20 plotters. As it happened, von Kluge found his position undermined by a catastrophe of a different sort. On the 15th, when driving to visit his embattled troops in the Falaise pocket, he was inexplicably out of touch for 12 hours. As he explained shakily on his arrival at Eberbach's HQ, he had been caught in an artillery barrage. His radio had been knocked out and he had spent hours taking refuge in a ditch. Hitler came to the conclusion that von Kluge had been trying to contact the Allies in order to capitulate with all his forces. No evidence for his belief has ever come to light, but Hitler was clearly eager to dispense with yet another general who had proved himself

A British soldier checks for mines in the hedgerows and grass verges on the outskirts of Falaise

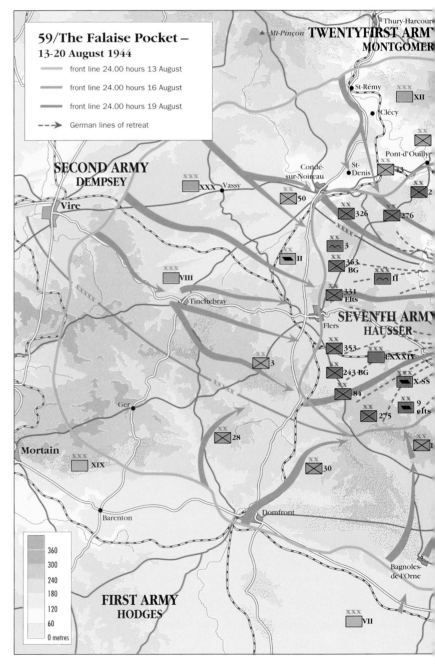

59/The Falaise Pocket –
13-20 August 1944

front line 24.00 hours 13 August

front line 24.00 hours 16 August

front line 24.00 hours 19 August

German lines of retreat

unworthy by his "lack of will," and by his failure to do the impossible. The following day, without informing von Kluge, he sent for Field-Marshal Walther Model from the Eastern Front, made him Supreme Commander West, and ordered von Kluge back to the HQ of the Fifth Panzer Army. There von Kluge at last proposed the withdrawal that would save the Seventh Army. Hitler agreed to pull them back across the Orne, clearly hoping Model could work a miracle.

With the Americans in place at Argentan and the Canadians and Poles moving so slowly, it was now too late to close the gap between Argentan and Falaise.

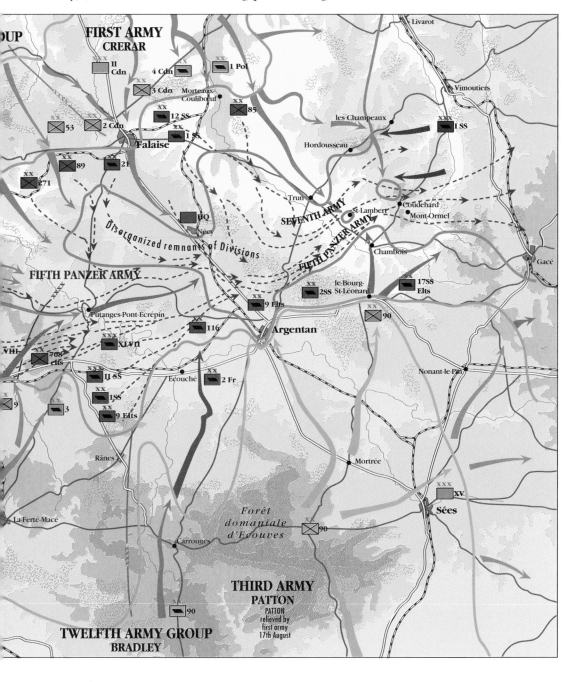

The aftermath of the battle – a typical road in the Argentan area littered with wrecked vehicles and the dead of von Kluge's broken army

The link-up would have to come further east, between Trun and Chambois. In effect, Bradley was now committed to precisely what he wished to avoid, both a short left hook and a long encirclement. No one deliberately chose to create the gap. It and its belated closure were the product of compromises, errors of judgement, and personal and cultural differences, all compounded by the speed at which events happened. They were all consequences of the fog of war – the misunderstandings and improvisations that attend upon large-scale operations.

On the 17th two armored divisions – the 4th Canadian and 1st Polish Armoured – crossed the River Dives some 10 miles east of Falaise and drove southeast along the river. By that evening, as the Americans took another step northwards, the gap between the two forces was just six miles.

Within this 20-by-10-mile pocket, with its narrowing neck, were 100,000 Germans. Bombed and shelled continuously, they had little left with which to fight and no chance of reinforcements. Their only escape was along the few narrow roads leading through Chambois and St-Lambert.

Technically, escape was not yet an option and it was certainly not an option that von Kluge was free to take, as he learned brutally with Model's sudden and unannounced arrival on the 17th. Von Kluge's final order from Hitler was to go home but always to leave word as to his whereabouts, a sure sign he could expect arrest for his complicity in the July 20 plot. It was the end, professionally and personally. The next day he wrote a final note to Hitler telling him the military reality as he saw it – and as it proved to be – though not recanting his faith in the Führer himself, let alone finding fault with the lunacy that had led to such needless destruction. "The German people have borne so much it is time to put an end to this frightfulness. Show yourself great enough to put an end to a hopeless struggle," he wrote. On his way home, near Metz, he took a poisoned capsule.

Model, meanwhile, had seen at once the desperate plight of the trapped forces. He ordered an immediate withdrawal through the Argentan–Falaise gap and across the Dives, an operation that would take four days. To keep the gap open the 2nd SS Panzer Corps attempted to cut off the Canadians in Trun. It was a hopeless gesture, for two days later Polish tanks fought their way to the top of a ridge overlooking Chambois. Below them they could see a terrible victory brewing.

A thousand vehicles – cars, armored cars, half-tracks, tanks, horse-drawn wagons and gun-carriages – packed the main road, backing up bumper to bumper into minor roads. That was just the beginning, for behind feeding into the exit were thousands more vehicles and foot-soldiers by the 10,000, all pressing into the death-trap. Above, Allied fighter-bombers ranged at will, flying 2,000–3,000 sorties a day. Already the exit was so clogged that the columns could hardly move.

On the same day, the 19th, the Canadians, after taking Trun, moved on to within two miles of Chambois while from the south the American 90th Division and 2nd French Armoured crowded in on the village. There that evening the leading units of the two forces – the 10th Polish Mounted Rifles and the U.S. 90th Division – finally met.

It was still, however, a permeable barrier. The few remaining 2nd SS Panzers held open the roads for the battered, crawling columns. Tanks, guns, transports and German troops created a "turkey-shoot" unmatched since Hitler's Blitzkrieg on Russia, and unmatched again until the retreat of Iraqi forces in the last days of the Gulf War.

One eyewitness, Sergeant-Major Erich Braun of the 2nd Panzer Division, recalled later being numbed by sights that were the stuff of nightmare. He wrote, "Anyone dying on top of those rolling steel coffins was just pitched overboard, so that a living man could take his place. The never-ending detonations, soldiers waving to us, begging for help – the dead, their faces still screwed up in agony, huddled everywhere in trenches and shelters – the officers and men who had lost their nerve, burning vehicles from which piercing screams could be heard and men, driven crazy, crying, shouting, swearing, laughing hysterically – and the horses, some still harnessed to the shafts, screaming terribly, trying to escape the slaughter on the stumps of their hind legs." Only the pall hanging like the smoke of a huge funeral pyre above the columns offered any protection against the rockets and bullets of the Typhoons and P-47 Thunderbolts. The wounded were huddled in groups, awaiting captivity. Every remaining building was crammed with men seeking protection and rest.

At dawn on the 20th an attempt by Hausser's tanks to force open a second escape route ended in confusion and only added to the tangle of flaming wreckage. Troops fled eastwards on foot. Horses were left to their fate, still in harness. Within the neck, a little pocket of resistance remained intact in the southern part of the village of St-Lambert, where some of the 2nd Panzer fought back against the Canadians of the South Alberta Regiment, part of the 4th Armored, in the northern half. There the main square had been held by a single Panther which knocked out 14 Canadian tanks. It was silenced when a lieutenant climbed on it, just at the moment the tank's commander emerged. The two fought hand-to-hand until the German was shot by an infantryman and the lieutenant tossed a grenade into the open turret. To clear the rest of the Germans the commander, Major David Currie, who was later awarded a VC, called in artillery fire on the whole village –

A wounded sergeant stoically awaits his fate

ordering his men to find what cover they could – and on the German columns approaching from the Dives. Shells whistled down on the armor, infantry and horses with terrible results. Horses panicked, stampeding with their wagons and guns through hedges and down the banks, clogging the river crossing with dead and dying animals, dead and dying men, and wrecked equipment.

The St-Lambert corridor slammed shut that evening but small groups of men and vehicles sneaked through Allied lines by night. Most of the generals made it out. Hausser escaped wounded in a tank and Meyer, whose famous 12th Panzers, once 20,000 strong, were now reduced to 100, forced a French civilian to lead him to freedom.

On the 21st, the 2nd Panzer Corps made one final effort to shift the Poles from the ridge above Chambois but without success. The next day the German tanks were ordered back. All resistance died, the gap closed for good and the Allied troops moved into the silent pocket, seeing scenes beyond imagination.

The pathetic remnants of the Seventh Army and Fifth Panzers left behind 50,000 men in captivity and 10,000 dead, along with some 500 tanks and assault guns. The additional hardware they abandoned was awe-inspiring. On the U.S. side of the battlefield were 700 artillery pieces and 5,000 vehicles. On the British side were 1,800 trucks and 669 cars – more than 9,000 pieces of equipment in total.

Hundreds of German prisoners on the move towards a collection point watched over by American troops and medics

American troops celebrate the victory with relieved and happy French civilians

These wrecked remnants were nothing compared to the sights and the abominable stench of this, one of the worst killing fields of the war. The main battle sites around Trun, St-Lambert and Chambois were covered with dead soldiers, dead horses, dead cattle, all packed between the wrecks of vehicles. In the shimmering heat, flesh decayed quickly. Bluebottles hummed, and bodies, grossly swollen by gas, crawled with maggots. Men donned gas-masks to walk amongst the carnage, deflating the bloated carcasses with bursts of fire. Hundreds of feet above, the pilots of observation aircraft recoiled at the smell. When Eisenhower visited the place two days after the battle was over, he was appalled. He wrote, "I was conducted through it on foot, to encounter scenes that could only be described by Dante. It was literally possible to walk for hundreds of yards at a time stepping on nothing but dead and decaying flesh."

One group-captain, Desmond Scott, provided one of the most graphic accounts: "Bits of uniform were plastered to shattered tanks and trucks, and human remains hung in grotesque shapes on the blackened hedgerows. Corpses lay in pools of dried blood, staring into space and as if their eyes were being forced from their sockets. Two gray-clad bodies, both minus their legs, leaned against a clay bank as if in prayer. Strangely enough, it was the fate of the horses that upset me most. Harnessed as they were, it had been impossible for them to escape, and they lay in tangled heaps, their large wide eyes crying out to me in anguish. It was a sight that pierced the soul."

It was the Germans' greatest defeat since Stalingrad. It could have been worse. The gap might have been closed five days earlier. The Americans could only have moved faster by drawing on other forces driving eastwards to the Seine, but Montgomery had not reinforced Simonds as he might have done, and historians now agree that the Canadians might have made an impenetrable barrier along the Dives with quicker and more devastating results. All the German generals might have been taken. There might have been a formal surrender with the capture of up to 100,000 men. As it was, about a third of the Seventh Army - between 20,000 and 40,000 men - escaped. The impact on German morale, though great, might have been much greater.

In the end, perhaps, it didn't matter. Allied victory in the West was certain - doubly so because an Anglo–American force had landed in the south of France and was quickly moving north. The troops that escaped had little left with which to fight - of seven armored divisions, just 1,300 men, 24 tanks and 60 artillery pieces managed to cross the Seine. On the day the the Falaise pocket closed, bringing an end to the campaign in Normandy except for outposts of resistance in St Malo and Brest, the American Third Army was already over the Seine.

As Bradley had predicted, the road to Paris and to the German frontier was open.

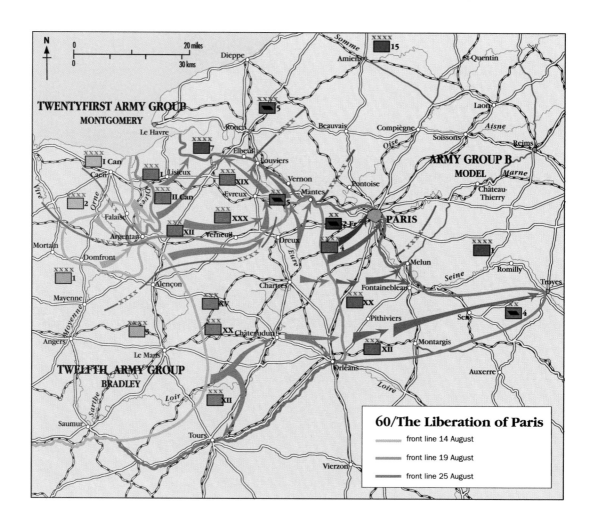

60/The Liberation of Paris

front line 14 August

front line 19 August

front line 25 August

The joy of liberty – and the crowds go wild in what is again "Gay Paree" as they welcome the Free French and Allied troops into Paris

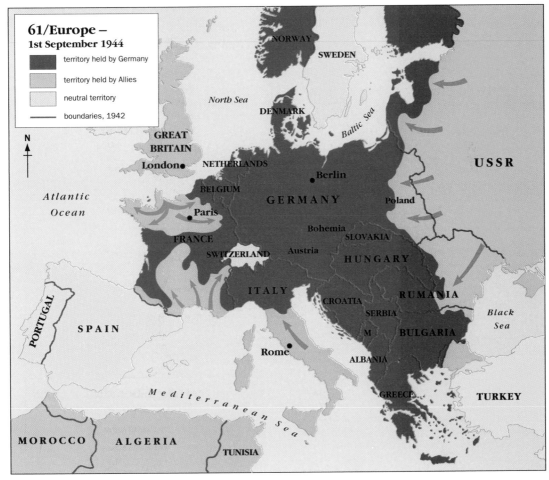

61/Europe –
1st September 1944

- territory held by Germany
- territory held by Allies
- neutral territory
- —— boundaries, 1942

N

NORWAY

SWEDEN

North Sea

DENMARK

Baltic Sea

GREAT
BRITAIN

London

NETHERLANDS

Berlin

BELGIUM

Atlantic
Ocean

GERMANY

Poland

USSR

Paris

FRANCE

Bohemia

SLOVAKIA

SWITZERLAND

Austria

HUNGARY

ITALY

CROATIA

RUMANIA

SERBIA

Black
Sea

PORTUGAL

SPAIN

M

BULGARIA

Rome

ALBANIA

Mediterranean Sea

GREECE

TURKEY

MOROCCO

ALGERIA

TUNISIA

One of the many Allied casualties of the fighting in Normandy. Although only a temporary memorial, this touchingly shows the growing respect and gratitude the French felt for their liberators

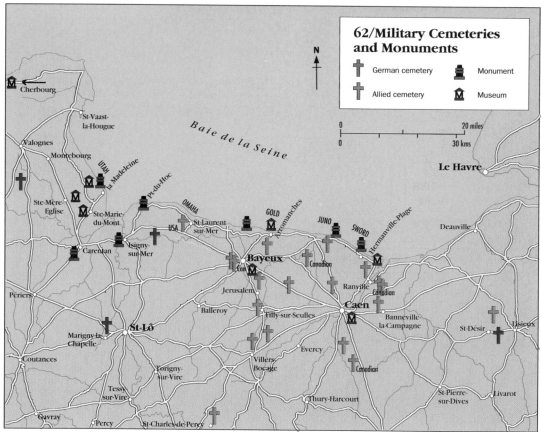

62/Military Cemeteries and Monuments

N

✝ German cemetery   🏛 Monument

✝ Allied cemetery   Ⓜ Museum

| 0 | | | 20 miles |
| 0 | | | 30 kms |

Baie de la Seine

Cherbourg
St-Vaast-la-Hougue
Valognes
Montebourg
UTAH
la Madeleine
Ste-Mère-Eglise
Ste-Marie-du-Mont
Pt-du-Hoc
OMAHA
St-Laurent-sur-Mer
GOLD
Aromanches
JUNO
SWORD
Hermanville-Plage
Le Havre
Deauville
USA
Carentan
Isigny-sur-Mer
Bayeux
Canadian
Ranville
Canadian
Périers
Jerusalem
Caen
Banneville-la-Campagne
St-Désir
Lisieux
Balleroy
Tilly-sur-Seulles
St-Lô
Marigny-la-Chapelle
Evercy
Canadian
Coutances
Villers-Bocage
Torigny-sur-Vire
Thury-Harcourt
St-Pierre-sur-Dives
Livarot
Tessy-sur-Vire
Gavray
Percy
St-Charles-de-Percy

Allied and German Command Hierarchies

Allied Command for Operation *Overlord*

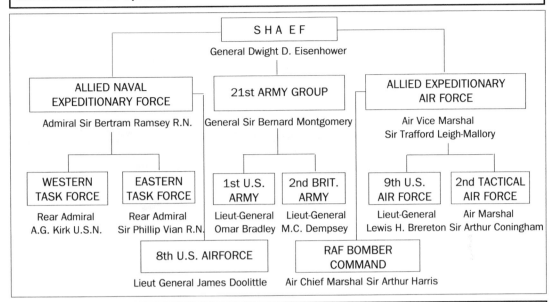

SHAEF
General Dwight D. Eisenhower

ALLIED NAVAL EXPEDITIONARY FORCE
Admiral Sir Bertram Ramsey R.N.

21st ARMY GROUP
General Sir Bernard Montgomery

ALLIED EXPEDITIONARY AIR FORCE
Air Vice Marshal Sir Trafford Leigh-Mallory

WESTERN TASK FORCE
Rear Admiral A.G. Kirk U.S.N.

EASTERN TASK FORCE
Rear Admiral Sir Phillip Vian R.N.

1st U.S. ARMY
Lieut-General Omar Bradley

2nd BRIT. ARMY
Lieut-General M.C. Dempsey

9th U.S. AIR FORCE
Lieut-General Lewis H. Brereton

2nd TACTICAL AIR FORCE
Air Marshal Sir Arthur Coningham

8th U.S. AIRFORCE
Lieut General James Doolittle

RAF BOMBER COMMAND
Air Chief Marshal Sir Arthur Harris

Allied Command in Northwest Europe, Fall 1944 (Ground Forces only)

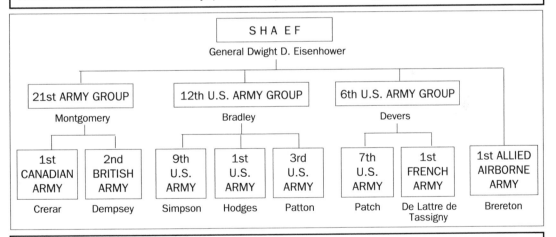

SHAEF
General Dwight D. Eisenhower

21st ARMY GROUP
Montgomery

12th U.S. ARMY GROUP
Bradley

6th U.S. ARMY GROUP
Devers

1st CANADIAN ARMY
Crerar

2nd BRITISH ARMY
Dempsey

9th U.S. ARMY
Simpson

1st U.S. ARMY
Hodges

3rd U.S. ARMY
Patton

7th U.S. ARMY
Patch

1st FRENCH ARMY
De Lattre de Tassigny

1st ALLIED AIRBORNE ARMY
Brereton

German High Command in the West, June 1944

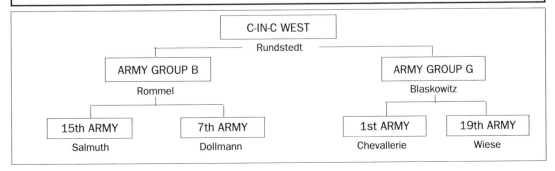

C-IN-C WEST
Rundstedt

ARMY GROUP B
Rommel

ARMY GROUP G
Blaskowitz

15th ARMY
Salmuth

7th ARMY
Dollmann

1st ARMY
Chevallerie

19th ARMY
Wiese

Chronology

23 January	Eisenhower gives final approval to Montgomery's plan for the proposed Normandy landings
7–8 April	Presentation of the *Overlord* plan at St Paul's given by Montgomery
3 June	Troops embarked
4 June	Weather conditions force D-Day postponement
	D-Day confirmed for 6 June
6 June	Allied landings begin
7 June	Bayeux, first city in France to be liberated
12 June	U.S. troops fighting from Utah and Omaha meet near Carentan
14 June	7th Armoured Division driven back from attacks on Villers-Bocage and Hill 213
18–21 June	The "Great Storm" in the Channel destroys Mulberry harbor at St-Laurent and severely disrupts supplies
18 June	German forces in northern Cotentin Peninsula cut off by U.S. VII Corps
25 June	*Operation Epsom* launched across the Odon valley southwest of Caen
27 June	Cherbourg garrison surrenders to U.S. forces
30 June	Last German forces holding out in north Cotentin surrender
8 July	*Operation Charnwood* launched, preceeded by carpet-bombing, XXX Corps launched their attack on Caen
10 July	British and Canadians occupy Caen
17 July	Rommel wounded in fighter-bomber attack and is replaced by von Kluge
18 July	*Operation Goodwood* launched. Americans capture St-Lô
20 July	Hilter wounded in Stauffenberg bomb plot
25 July	*Operation Cobra* launched, preceeded by carpet-bombing by 1,500 heavy bombers
30 July	*Operation Bluecoat* launched towards Aunay-sur-Odon and Vire
1 August	Bradley assumes command of Twelth Army Group, Hodges takes command U.S. First Army, Patton's Third Army activated.
7 August	Germans launch *Operation Lüttich*, the Mortain counterattack *Operation Totalize* launched towards Falaise
12 August	U.S. Third Army under Patton capture Alençon
14 August	*Operation Tractable* launched and Falaise captured
17 August	Model takes over command of German Armies in the west and orders full retreat from the Allied encirclement
19 August	Polish, Canadian and American Divisions meet across the neck of the Falaise Pocket
21 August	The Falaise Gap is closed
25 August	Paris liberated by American and French forces
1 September	Eisenhower assumes command of all Allied ground forces

Codenames

Anvil	The first name for Allied landings in the south of France, August 1944
Arcadia	The Washington Conference, December 1941 – January 1942
Bodyguard	Cover and deception plan for Allied strategy in Europe
Bombardon	Floating steel component of breakwaters to seaward of the Mulberry harbors
Bluecoat	British attack towards Aunay-sur-Odon, 30 July
Charnwood	British and Canadian attack on Caen, 8 July
Cobra	American break out near St-Lô, 25–29 July
Crossbow	Allied measures against attacks by V-1 flying bombs
Dragoon	Final name for *Anvil* – see above
Epsom	Second Army's operation to cross the Odon and Orne rivers southwest of Caen, 26 June – 1 July
Eureka	The Teheran Conference, November 1943
Fortitude	Cover plan for *Operation Overlord*
Goodwood	Second Army's attack southeast of Caen, 18–21 July
Gooseberry	Artificial breakwater for the offshore anchorages and Mulberry harbors
Lüttich	German counterattack at Mortain, 7 August
Mulberrry	Artificial harbor off the Normandy coast
Neptune	Naval assault phase of *Operation Overlord*
Overlord	Allied campaign in northwest Europe, 1944–45
Phoenix	Concrete caisson for Mulberry breakwaters
Pluto	Pipeline under the ocean, scheme to supply petrol from England to the Continent
Totalize	First Canadian Army's attack towards Falaise, Phase I 8–11 August
Tractable	First Canadian Army's attack towards Falaise, Phase II 14–16 August
Ultra	Intelligence from the interception and decryption of enemy cyphers by Britain's Code and Cypher School, Bletchley Park

Index

Map page references are shown
in **bold** typeface
Photograph page references are
shown in *italic* typeface

Index

Abbreviations on Maps

(BG)	Battle Group
Div	Division
elts	elements of
GAF ⎱ LW ⎰	Luftwaffe, Infantry, Division
Pz	Panzer
Pz Gd	Panzer Grenadiers
recce	reconnaissance
W	(Werfer) Mortar Brigade

Bibliography

Ambrose, Stephen
The Supreme Commander,
London, 1970
Bradley, Omar
A Soldier's Story, New York,
1951; London, 1952
A General's Life, New York,
1983
Collins, J. Lawton
Lightning Joe, Louisiana,
1979
Cruikshank, Charles
Deception in World War II,
Oxford, 1979 and 1981
D'Este, Carlo
Decision in Normandy,
London, 1983
Eisenhower, Dwight
Crusade in Europe,
New York, 1948
Fraser, Sir David
*Knight's Cross: A Biography
of Field-Marshal Erwin
Rommel*, London, 1993
Hamilton, Nigel
*Montgomery: Master of the
Battlefield*, London, 1983
Hastings, Max
*Overlord: D-Day and the
Battle for Normandy*,
London, 1984
Haswell, J.
*The Intelligence and
Deception of the D-Day
Landings*, London, 1979
Holt, Tonie
*The Visitor's Guide to the
Normandy Landing
Beaches*, Ashbourne,
Derbyshire, 1989, Edison, NJ,
1989
How, Major J.J.
*Normandy: The British
Breakout*, London, 1981
Keegan, John
Six Armies in Normandy,
London and New York, 1982
Lewin, Ronald
*Montgomery as Military
Commander*, London, 1971

*Rommel as Military
Commander*, New York,
1977
Ultra Goes to War, London,
1978
McKee, Alexander
Caen: Anvil of Victory,
London, 1964
Miller, Russell
Nothing Less Than Victory,
London, 1993
Montgomery, Field Marshal
Viscount
Memoirs, London, 1958
Normandy to the Baltic,
London, 1947
Patton, George
War As I Knew It, Boston,
1947; London, 1948
Ryan, Cornelius
The Longest Day, New York,
1959; London 1961
Shirer, William
*The Rise and Fall of the
Third Reich*, New York and
London, 1960
Speidel, Hans
We Defended Normandy,
London, 1951
Stagg, James M.
Forecast for Overlord,
London, 1971
Tute, Warren, John Costello and
Terry Hughes
D-Day,
London, 1974 and 1975
Weigley, Russell F.
Eisenhower's Lieutenants,
Bloomington, Indiana, 1981
Wertenbaker, Charles Christian
Invasion!, New York, 1944
Wilmot, Chester
The Struggle for Europe,
London, 1952

Picture Credits

With grateful acknowledgement to